*Northwestern University Publications
in Analytical Philosophy*

Motive
AND
Intention

An Essay in
the Appreciation of Action

Roy Lawrence

Northwestern University Press

EVANSTON · 1972

*Roy Lawrence is Law and Humanities Fellow,
The Law School, The University of Chicago*

*We can make several things clearer,
but we cannot make anything clear.*

RAMSEY

Contents

Foreword

THIS BRILLIANT AND SUBTLE WORK challenges, and indeed quite demolishes, some conceptual schemes that have long been important to philosophy, ethics, and jurisprudence. So powerful have those ideas been that they are still, as the author of this work points out, widely regarded as conventional wisdom.

What is at issue is how certain familiar forms of human action are to be understood. Traditionally the models invoked, consciously or otherwise, have been Platonic and Cartesian, even in the cases of thinkers who have been unaware of any debt to those sources. Gilbert Ryle's great work *The Concept of Mind* did not abolish them; indeed, it betrayed some of their still potent influence.

In these pages Lawrence examines with minute care a family

of concepts that are constantly used, both in historical narrative and in everyday speech, for the understanding of human action. Examples of such concepts are those of 'motive', 'purpose', 'intention', and so on. His aim is to make them more clearly understood, not by cramming them into preconceived theories of human nature, but phenomenologically; that is, by close examination and by considering with care and an open mind how they actually function, in historical explanation, for example. If at times the reader feels he is losing touch with the author's thought, this will not be the result of obscurity in the work itself. It is in fact rare to find philosophical thought expressed with such clarity and economy. Rather, it is apt to be because he has lost sight of the author's overall purpose. That purpose can perhaps best be understood in the light of a certain pattern in the history of thought.

Thus, if we somewhat artificially distinguish men from nature, we can note that philosophers, and men generally, have always found it easier to think of nature than to think of themselves. They therefore try to understand themselves in terms of things quite different, but easier to grasp, and the resulting theories are crude. The mind, for example, is thought of as something within, which acts upon the body; or it is conceived as a kind of director, governor, sometimes almost as a puppeteer. Sometimes a third thing, the will, is introduced to serve as liaison between the governing mind and the passively responding body. The metaphors borrowed from physical nature to describe mental activity are so numerous that it is difficult to talk philosophically without them. Thus, the mind weighs reasons; it ponders; it throws light on this or that; it sees the point; it pursues trains of thought and follows a chain of reasoning; it grasps this or that idea, portrays things in imagination and stores them in memory; and so on, endlessly.

Philosophical theories have not escaped the distorting influence of such patterns and metaphors. It is in fact fairly common to find thinkers of considerable reputation speaking blithely of volitions, and assigning to them the role of moving the body this way and that; or of ideas and purposes causing a man to behave as he does; or of motives, purposes, intentions, choices, wishes, desires, and acts of will, as though these were all just diverse names for the same thing, conceived as an inner perturbation of the spirit that causes a bodily motion. Though a man with minimal learning should know better, even philosophers sometimes find it natural to think of themselves as inhabiting their bodies, and using their limbs as instruments for the manipulation of things outside, and are apt to have the feeling of achieving understanding when they can represent their own behavior as the consequence of certain transactions between body and mind.

This whole conception of human nature was urged by Plato, who took the crudest ideas of vulgar understanding and crystallized them into a philosophical system which few of his philosophical descendants have been able to shake off. In such a system we find ourselves enabled to think in ways that are familiar, and at the same time philosophical, and are thus beguiled into thinking we have achieved enlightenment, when in fact we have only intellectualized vulgarity, thereby reducing our embarrassment at our own ignorance.

The Cartesian philosophy brought this approach to its culmination, and even thinkers who are aware of no debt to Descartes, and in fact strongly repudiate him, are often still under his spell. It was central to Cartesian philosophy to explain human action in terms of the inner workings of the soul, and there are still thinkers who can with a perfectly straight face suggest that a man may be quite literally caused to act in certain ways by the intentions or motives transpiring inside him.

Noting the strange and somewhat esoteric character of such descriptions, as well as their practical fruitlessness, some theoreticians, particularly in empirical psychology, have gone to the opposite extreme of trying to expunge such concepts as 'motive' and 'purpose' from our thinking altogether. But this is only to be beguiled by the Platonic and Cartesian heritage in a different way, for the models at work are about the same as before. Instead, for example, of thinking of a rational human agent as a mind inside a body, we are instead led to think of men somewhat in the manner in which we think of clocks, with the traditional ideas of cause and effect as deeply entrenched as ever.

What Lawrence bids us do, then, is this: to be true to what we actually find and not defer to fond notions. It is a worthy cause, both in the interest of arriving at clearer understanding of ourselves, and for the sheer delight of precise and subtle thought, gracefully expressed. No philosophical work has ever settled anything once for all. Some, nevertheless, cannot be ignored. Even those, for example, who reject the basic themes of Gilbert Ryle's *The Concept of Mind* cannot just barge ahead in disregard of it. Similarly, I think it is fair to say that whoever henceforth, for a long time to come, undertakes to discuss motives, purposes, and intentions philosophically cannot do so in disregard of Lawrence's work, except at his peril.

RICHARD TAYLOR

Preface

THIS IS A CONTRIBUTION to the phenomenology of human activity, an attempt to understand our understanding of ourselves. Parts of this examination are polemical; I believe certain of the concepts underlying our judgments of conduct have been remarkably, even coherently, misrepresented by other writers. If there is any novelty of technique in this work, it is only the frequent citation of substantive accounts of particular actions. There is no deep insight provoking this selective display of evidence how actually we appreciate the nature and quality of our acts. My hope is a positive one, that such analysis and mere fact as follow provide a usable sketch of real affairs, and not for philosophers alone. (Even if the work has such utility, Robert Lowell's formula for poets may fit here, too: half-balmy, and over-accoutered.)

I can testify to the occasional criticism and steady encouragement of my colleagues Elizabeth Anscombe, Vere Chappell, and Alan Donagan. I cannot claim affiliation for this work, in substance or style, with that of John Austin. Still, he is remembered, with gratitude.

Motive
and Intention

I

What Motives Are

Part One

WHEN SPEAKING OF A MAN'S INTENTIONS, we sometimes indicate their quality, for example, honorable. Sometimes also we say what his intention is or was; we identify it. To do this we use an expression, such as a verb in the infinitive, which signifies an action or achievement. This shows that intentions are actions (at least, of a kind).

Yet there is a very strong inclination to deny this. We want to construe the concept differently, to internalize it. Philosophically, it is standard practice to talk of intentions as though they were the mental *associates* of certain actions. One then asks what specifically intentions are and just what their relation is to their associated actions. It would be better to ask what in a man's intentions distinguishes them from his other actions.

My aim here is to examine certain problems concerning 'intention', 'motive', and related concepts. The point of depar-

3

ture, for convenience, will be three statements to be made concerning 'intention', 'motive', and 'purpose'. These statements may be treated as summary descriptions. To see whether they fit the facts will require an appreciation of certain common situations and of familiar ways of describing and explaining human activities. Wrongly construed, such descriptions and explanations are among the sources of disagreement in this region of the philosophy of mind. In the nature of the case, then, no such formulas as those to be given could be supposed to state pure discoveries. They are efforts to dispel the attraction of a contrary view which is persistent and respectable.

To conceive of intentions, motives, and purposes in a way which preserves both what distinguishes them from one another and what connects them, we can start with these approximations:

(i) an intention (for the future) is an action in prospect;

(ii) a motive is a circumstance because of which one may take (certain) action;

(iii) a purpose is a desired condition seen as achievable.

These statements are meant just to express my conviction that one's pre-theoretical conception of human motives, plans, purposes, and the like is *not* (necessarily) that of present states of the individual. In what follows I shall argue, to the contrary, that it is one of future (or, in the case of some motives, past and present) activities, powers, acquisitions, accomplishments, personal relations, etc.

I shall not be much concerned here with internal differences among this group. Typical differences are recognized in daily life, however, and they can be stated in terms compatible with (i)–(iii). For example, an account of someone's jumping a fence might be taken to advert indifferently to the actor's motive and to his intention in so doing. But the undertaking *is* viewed differently according as one speaks of the actor's intention or of his motive. In the simple case suggested, his intention is the achievement of that height, his motive (improbably) its achievement seen as desirable. The general characterizations offered in (i) and (ii) reflect this difference.

Similarly for purpose and intention: is it possible even in simple cases to make out a real difference? To adapt the example, suppose someone is evidently about to jump a fence, that he is asked why, and that the question is taken as one about the whole enterprise, rather than some aspect of it ("Why do that?" as against "Why not look for a stile?"). A likely answer to the question, so taken, could be "To take a shortcut home." Now, does this response cite indifferently the intention and the purpose of the act? How the issue is settled depends upon the need for distinction in a given context. Thus, if there were a need to mark it, a difference would be made manifest in how the response was understood. The man's intention in jumping the fence is to (put himself in a position to) take a certain way home, understood to be shorter. His purpose is to shorten the way.

Still, it may be supposed that our experience does offer a kind of action in which intention and purpose coincide. That would be an episode in which the actor has nothing in mind beyond the deed itself, for example, leaping the fence just from exuberance. But such a case will not bear that interpretation. Here the episode is so described that no purpose can be elicited for it. It has none. Thus if one asks the actor why he did it, the question will likely be refused application. Accordingly there is a difference preserved, a distinction made available, in the contrast of (i) and (iii). A person's intention is that which he is to do (perhaps through doing a prior act), his purpose, there being one, that which he is to achieve by so doing.

It will be assumed in what follows that (iii) is the least contentious of those three statements. The other two are of equal interest, since the notion of 'intention' and that of 'motive' are subject to similar abuse, and for similar reasons, by philosophers and others. It will be convenient here, and for the remainder of this chapter, to give a foundation for (ii), the statement on 'motive'. We shall work our way backward in that formula, examining first the sense of the words "because of which" as they occur there, and then of "a circumstance."

It would make little difference to substitute the words "in recognition" for "because," as it occurs in (ii). In contrast, it would make a significant difference to change "because" to "in consequence." Similarly, the use of the phrase "because of which" has an important advantage over that of such an apparent alternative as the phrase "which is the reason why." Use of the latter expression would risk the loss of an essential discrimination. It would indeed be true to say that to give someone's motive for a particular piece of behavior is to give the reason why he so behaved, or might well so behave. But giving

(a) *the reason why* he so behaved (or might so behave) is less definite than giving

(b) *his reason for* so behaving.

The role of the word "reason" in (a) is that which it has in its generic sense. We may call its more specific use as in (b) the use of the *possessive* sense of 'reason for doing such-and-such a thing'; (b) is, as it were, a determinant of (a). That (b) is more definite than (a) should be apparent from inspection. Consider the difference between the first pair below, examples of (a), and the second pair, examples of (b).

(i) Coalitions find it possible to agree, as a rule, only on what not to do. This is *the reason why* their tendency is so often to do nothing at all.

(ii) Stalin persisted far too long in a line of policy which was jeopardizing the very existence of the Chinese Communist Party. *The reason for* this, apparently, was the fact that the matter became a prestige issue between him and his rivals in Russia.

(iii) The revolt of non-Europe against Europe was indeed destined to be the dominant political reality of the middle decades of the present century. And Stalin *had some reason* to feel that he ought, by right, to be the proprietor of this process.

(iv) Stalin . . . *had powerful reason* to fear an insurgent victory in Spain, particularly a quick and dramatic one.[1]

Note that to assign the first pair to (a) is not to imply that they are not instances of (b). It is unlikely that they are, but this improbability is in each case a matter of something additional, for example, whether or not the struggle among the Russian leaders *warranted* Stalin's so treating the Chinese.

---

1. G. F. Kennan, *Russia and the West under Lenin and Stalin* (Boston, 1960), pp. 45, 273, 274–275, and 309 (emphasis added).

I have deliberately chosen, as examples of attribution of possession of a reason for doing something, statements about having reason to *feel* and reason to *fear*. This is in order to indicate the scope of (b), in which the essential stress is on possession of a reason and not, say, on that for which it is a reason. It is indifferent here whether, by some appropriate criterion, having reason to feel or to fear is considered derivative from a basic case of having reason to act.

7

Thus our characterization of motives, when it is applied, is meant to be interpreted in the light of this fact: to give someone's motive for an action is to give *his* reason, the reason he possesses, for that action. Of those several reasons we might correctly adduce in explanation of someone's conduct on a given occasion, only those that are his reasons are called the motives of his conduct.[2] This is a boundary for our concept of a motive.

Some notice must be given to one common type of explanation by appeal to a reason possessed. That type is exemplified in saying that Talleyrand's reason for entering the Church was that, having a limp, he was unfit for a military career. Prima facie, to concede this, that often we say a man's reason *for* doing one thing was that he could *not* do a preferred alternative, should be disconcerting. But it does seem plain, and acceptable, that we construe such explanations as elliptical. What is elided is a statement of the actor's full plan, of which the actual realization was limited by circumstance to a second-best disjunct. In Talleyrand's case, then, his reason for entering the Church was that, having decided to enter some one of the conventional aristocratic services, he realized the Church was his only such opportunity. His reason for doing the one thing is *not* fully identified with the reason why he did not do the other.

Since it is thus a routine and striking practice on our part to attribute to another person possession of a reason for acting,

2. To avoid confusion, it is well to note that when, faced by something already done, we ask for the actor's reason, we do not thereby concede that whatever he can truly claim to have *thought* to be reason for so acting is in fact such. That is, in speaking of his reason we sometimes mean only to indicate what he had in mind as seeming occasion for action. To indicate such is not to grant that he truly had (that as) reason so to act.

it is desirable to make plain what this common notion of 'possessing' a reason does not amount to.

First, to say of someone that he has (a) reason to take a certain action is not to say that, necessarily, he *knows* that this is so. It is one thing to distinguish within the universe of reasons for a given human action one (if there be such) which is a motive of the action. It is something different, and subordinate, to discriminate between

    (b′) a reason he has for a given course of action and
           knows that he has

and

    (b″) a reason he has but does *not* know that he has.

That is, one may be led to ask whether (b′) or (b″) obtains in a given case by the fact that to attribute to someone a reason to do so-and-so is not necessarily thereby to advert to any belief, knowledge, or assumption on his part concerning that reason. Consider the reason why the patriarch who had full reason to call for a vendetta did not do so — none dared tell him of his daughter's abduction. He did not know of the reason he had to act. A further distinction, worth noting in this context, is that between

    (b′1) knowing of (that circumstance which is) the reason
           one has to take a certain action

and

    (b′2) knowing of that circumstance *as* reason for so doing.

A possession is often a gift. What is it to give someone a motive? To one drawn to the wrong theoretical picture, a likely first answer is this wrong answer: to give someone a motive is somehow to make him cognizant of the circumstances which constitute the motive. Or, for a total failure, this: to provoke within him a certain operative agitation.

Why is even the first of these, the better one, still wrong?

For this reason, that neither to be a donor nor a possessor of a reason to act is it necessary that the possessor have any belief concerning the circumstances which constitute that reason. Take it positively, then. What is the nature of the reciprocity of giving and having (a certain) motive to act? It is this: to give someone a motive to act is to create or embody a condition assignable to him as reason so to act.[3] I make you such a gift when, say, I deceive you. You come into possession of a certain motive when I deceive you. This is so whether or not you find me out, or even have the wit to wonder. Having a motive is like having a choice, not like having a pain.

In the light of this, we can see why the second sentence in the following is mistaken:

We can ask of a reason for an action "Was that his motive?". But we cannot ask of a motive, without in some way repeating ourselves, "Was that the reason why he did it?".[4]

The second sentence is mistaken, that is, if thought to hold true of the second question as asked on every occasion. For a counterexample, imagine that a particularly memorable abomination of Caligula's afforded his assassin a motive to kill him, yet that the man struck in ignorance of *that* reason but for a different one (say, because Caligula had made his horse a priest). Or, what is less likely, for no reason. Thus a student, learning of the existence of the first reason, may sensibly ask whether that *was* the motive of the act, that is, the reason *for which* the killer struck.

Now, what Peters says has a measure of nagging plausibility. It comes from a setting suggested for the second claim

3. Again, it is a different and derivative thing to 'give' another person motive to act by *informing* him of his possession of such a reason.
4. R. S. Peters, *The Concept of Motivation* (London, 1958), p. 28.

by the preceding one. That setting is one presumption, but not the only one, we could make as to the circumstances in which the first question is asked. We could take that setting to be one in which — knowing that the agent did have a certain condition as motive and with that knowledge having then asked "But *was* that his motive?" — we should in effect already have sought to settle the question whether he acted for the reason he (might have thought that he) had so to act. Then to ask the second question would be to repeat oneself, as Peters says.

A second denial which needs to be made about possession of a reason to act is simply this: that someone had a reason to act in a given way and yet was ignorant of the fact that he had such a reason implies neither that he did nor did not so act. Recall our patriarch. There may come to him, in the course of a vendetta he called for no (good) reason, the grievous pleasure of finding that he *had* a reason, from the beginning.

Here, then, is the sum of these differences. To say that a man had a certain reason to take a certain action (that is, a motive for doing it) is to say none of these:

  (a) that he knew it;
  (b) that, whether or not he knew it, he did take that action;
  (c) nor yet, even if he did know it (and know of it as reason for so acting) and did so act, that he acted for that reason.

We have finally to note another, but connected, use of "his reason for." I refer to those occasions when the possessive pronoun is stressed. This would be done to call attention to a weighty fact. On occasion, one man's reason to do whatever is in question is different from that which is another man's reason to do the same sort of thing. As before, this discrimination can be made without indicating whether either of them has in fact taken the respective circumstance as reason for acting. To say that such-and-such is *his* reason, therefore, is not thereby to say that it *is* (regarded by him as) his reason.

Part Two

The use of the noun "circumstance" in (ii) may seem careless, in that it is so nonspecific. Yet I regard its use, or that of something equally general, as indispensable. It is required for the representation of some plain facts. These are facts ignored, denied, or strangely rationalized by the standard theory of motives. That is the doctrine that motives are conditions, generally taken to be emotions, private to the person concerned, such that only he could be in a position to know of (the actual quality of) that condition, or such that only he could have immediate knowledge of any condition which for him is a motive. This theory ought to have only a genetic interest for us. Why was it devised at all? Why is it still accepted? Still, to say it is the received view is a serious admission. The theory does pull strongly at us, and so makes it hard to attain a position from which to *see* that this conception of motives as private episodes is false to one's experience.

Then put the theory to one side. Consider some actual attributions of motive. A familiar context in which such assignments are made is historians' narratives, especially those giving an explanation for a discrepancy between what given circumstances lead one to anticipate a certain person would do and what he is known to have done. Here is an unremarkable example.

The chief advisers of Henry did not scruple to connive at infractions of the proclamation [forbidding priestly marriages]. Both Cranmer and Cromwell favored the Reformation: the former was himself secretly married . . . while the latter, though, as a layman, without any such personal motive, was disposed to relax the strictness of the rule of celibacy.[5]

Here what is attributed to an individual — in this case, Cranmer — as a motive, is a civil condition, that of being both priest and married. It is immediately intelligible that such a condition should be motive for the actions described.

Consider another example of the attribution to an individual of a specified motive. In this example, too, the motive will be a condition which is thought, or insinuated, to account for the puzzling conduct in the context of circumstances regarded as not sufficient by themselves (given the person in question) to account for it.

In March of 1929, he [Warburg, of the International Acceptance Bank] called for a stronger Federal Reserve Policy and argued that if the present orgy of "unrestrained speculation" were not brought promptly to a halt there would ultimately be a disastrous collapse. This . . . would "bring about a general depression involving this whole country." Only Wall Street spokesmen who took the most charitable view of Warburg contented themselves with describing him as obsolete. . . . Others hinted that he had a motive — presumably a short position.[6]

As commonly, what is imputed to this man as motive for the act is a particular aspect of his relations with certain other members of his society. Again, as commonly, the alleged mo-

5. H. C. Lea, *The History of Sacerdotal Celibacy in the Christian Church* (1907; New York, 1957), p. 396.
6. J. K. Galbraith, *The Great Crash, 1929* (Boston, 1954), p. 77.

tive is a disturbing aspect of those developing relations. But note that it is not said to *be* the felt disturbance (exhilaration, emotion, or what have you) possibly provoked by the circumstances in question.

Here is a third case:

There were, of course, domestic motives [as well as considerations of international position] for Bismarck's colonial policy. Hamburg was on the point of entering the German customs-union at last; and colonial markets were perhaps held out to the Hamburg merchants as some compensation for the loss of their Free Trade privileges. There were wider grounds, too. Men everywhere . . . were talking about "the age of imperialism," and the Germans were anxious not to be left out. Colonies provided a new "national" cause [with which to discredit Bismarck's opponents in the Reichstag].[7]

This example is more complex than the previous pair in three respects, none of which affects the main point. One difference is that in this last account the motive (in the first instance) is not actually named. What is understandably implicit is that a motive of the policy, for Bismarck, was the insuring, or easing, of the surrender of those privileges. The other two differences are that here a plurality of motives is supplied for one course of action; and that these several circumstances are indifferently and unexceptionably called by the historian both "motives" and "grounds."

These three, quite ordinary, samples have this negative feature in common. In none of them is a particular imputed motive an internal condition of operative agitation.[8] What pos-

7. A. J. P. Taylor, *Bismarck, the Man and the Statesman* (New York, 1955), p. 215.
8. For better measure, here in five passages are ten more examples, and they too bear out the point:

itive features do these motives have in common, *qua* motives, other than that in all cases they were reasons possessed by the persons concerned for taking the action thus explained? None. Apart from this, what is a motive 'in itself'? Evidently, anything you like. It is an aberration, surely, to construe talk of a man's motive as (sometimes Aesopian) reference to a quasi-

---

[Stalin's] fundamental motive was the protection of his own personal position (Kennan, *Russia and the West,* p. 252).

The emperor had to avoid the appearance of a purely religious war while telling both the pope and his intimates that the ending of the schism was his true aim. Probably it was, but it is clear that the political motive — the creation of an irresistible imperial authority — was quite as important to him (G. R. Elton, *Reformation Europe, 1517-1559* [London, 1963], p. 243).

The constant repetition by historians of such catch-phrases as Tory or Wilkite "mobs" has of course tended to obscure the true nature of such disturbances and the fact that crowds taking part in them were both socially identifiable and were impelled by specific grievances and by motives other than those of loot or monetary gain (G. Rudé, *The Crowd in the French Revolution* [Oxford, 1960], p. 232).

The time eventually came when the burden of their political genesis returned to haunt the freedmen and destroy their future. That was the time when the two dominant operative motives of Radical Reconstruction, party advantage and sectional business interests, became inactive — the time when it became apparent that those mighty ends could better be served by abandoning the experiment and leaving the freedmen to shift for themselves (C. V. Woodward, *The Burden of Southern History* [New York, 1961], pp. 104-5).

To the Allies as a whole Gukovsky ascribed four major motives for intervention: the restoration of an Eastern Front, paramount until the armistice; the stamping out of Bolshevism at its source, which predominated after the armistice; the establishment of economic control over Russia; and, least important, the securing of zones of political influence in Russia (J. M. Thompson, "Allied and American Intervention in Russia, 1918-1921," in *Rewriting Russian History: Soviet Interpretations of Russia's Past,* ed. C. E. Black, 2d ed. [New York, 1962], p. 337).

metabolic process mediating stimulus and response. Or as reference to some prodromal moment of the act itself. Yet it is the usual aim of philosophical remarks on the subject to achieve something like a systematic exchange of inner disturbance for 'disturbing' circumstance. As one such attempt, there is Locke's general characterization of motives: "The motive for continuing in the same state or action, is only the present satisfaction in it; the motive to change is always some uneasiness: nothing setting us upon the change of state, or upon any new action, but some uneasiness. This is the great motive that works on the mind to put it upon action. . . ." [9]

This undeclared program is so nearly universal among theorists as to be conventional wisdom. It is a view, for instance, from which the allusion to Cranmer's marriage is seen as giving us only an external clue to the probable motive, not as telling us what really it was. His (consciousness of his) secret marriage, it will be said, happened to be the condition for his then coming to have, or be possessed by, the unnamed motive. Alternatively, it may be said, a realization of the new significance of his own marriage was the occasion for the mobilization of an already existing fear or desire.

9. *An Essay Concerning Human Understanding*, II.21, para. 29, ed. A. C. Fraser, 2 vols. (Oxford, 1894), I, 331. In citing this passage as an example, I am taking it straightforwardly, and so less favorably than one might. Jonathan Edwards carefully adulterates Locke's simplicity, giving Locke's characterization an approving, though questionable, interpretation. Things are said by Edwards to be motives to volition (*sic*). Since they are motives, it must be that they are "viewed *as good*," which "includes in its signification, the removal or avoiding of evil, or of that which is disagreeable and uneasy." It is agreeable to be rid of uneasiness. So, Mr. Locke "must be understood as supposing that the end or aim which governs in the volition or act of preference, is the avoiding or removal of that uneasiness" (*Freedom of the Will*, Pt. I, sec. 2, ed. Paul Ramsey [New Haven, 1957], pp. 142–43).

One part, then, of what is at issue here is the role played in explanatory narrative by certain terms, such as "fear," "hunger," and "vanity." Some, such as "hope," "anxiety," and "remorse," have been taken in the abstract to be the names of distinct kinds of passions, reactions of the organism which are variously registered in consciousness. Less problematically, others stand for physiological needs one may seek to fill, or for dispositions to behave in certain stylized ways. Internal perturbations may be postulated to account for the realization of such a disposition — the latest manifestation of a man's self-destructiveness, for example. There can be no dispute that such terms do have an essential occurrence in some narratives of human (and animal) history. To take one useful instance, it has been said that in the competition for adherents, early Christianity had the advantage over other religious cults and the philosophic schools in that it "supplied more effective motives" for good conduct, namely, "fear of God, as in Judaism, devotion to Jesus who had suffered in order that sinlessness might be within man's reach, and love for your fellow Christians." [10]

But action-explanations which refer to motives are not uniform. One surface difference worth respecting is that some such explanations make use of such terms, as above ("fear of," "devotion to," "love for," etc.), yet others do not. Our previous examples are of the sort that do not. The point of observing this unremarkable difference is to bring out a certain implication of the traditional view. That is, that motive-explanations of this latter sort must be regarded as formally defective, in containing ostensible reference to a motive without an appropriate auxiliary expression. It is implicit, in contrast, that an explanation may be well formed even if it makes *no* mention

10. A. D. Nock, *Conversion: The Old and the New in Religion from Alexander the Great to Augustine of Hippo* (Oxford, 1933), p. 219.

of any public circumstance as (somehow provocative of) motive. As an instance of this last kind, here is a summary explanation of the secession:

Under the stimulus of constant agitation the leaders of the southern branch of the Democracy [i.e., the Democratic Party] forbade the voters to elect a Republican President unless they wished him to preside over a shattered government. A number of voters sufficient to create a Republican majority in the Electoral College defied the prohibition. Then southerners, in a state of hypermotion, moved by pride, self-interest, a sense of honor and fear, rushed to action; they were numerous enough and effective enough to force secession.[11]

We have in hand now, from social histories, examples of three forms of motive-explanation. They have a natural alignment. There are those in which no mention is made of a psychological state or episode as the motive. In the middle fall those of the second sort we noted, in which an attribution of some psychological state is linked with mention (e.g.) of another person or an anticipated event. Then come those in which the inner state, by itself, is named as motive. I take it that appreciation of the first sort is necessary to finding the second two intelligible. Yet much of the history of moral psychology can be represented as giving primacy to the third category. And to one taking that as paradigm, it may appear a sure and welcome rationalization to hold that human motives are illuminatingly comprehended by some such disjunction as "appetite or aversion."

What is said in the next two chapters should help to show what leads one to take the standard view. Here, let us note

11. R. F. Nichols, *The Disruption of American Democracy* (New York, 1948), p. 516.

some consequences, for this last example, of such a move, apart from the first false step of noticing only the one sort of common motive-explanation. What, then, do we learn from such a passage as that referring to the motives of the secession leaders when we read it in order to understand the historical event? As we read it, do we recognize (or infer, or recall) that pride and the rest are parochial forms of appetite or aversion, and so for *that* reason accept the account as explaining the rush to action of these men? If so, most of us radically misconceive a major purpose in attempting to recover the past. On the view in question, historical narrative is a gratuitous confirmation of first principles. To record and explain the past would never be to tell what (at *that* time and place) happened nor why *it* took place, as and when it did.

On one account, then, of the role in motive-explanations of (e.g.) "ambition," the term is thrown out as a bridge by which we may pass from the idiosyncrasies of the given to some generic principle of human action. Or, at least, the action is typed as the known product of *one* kind of dynamic thought and feeling. But there is an account which seems better to fit the facts. That is, that a motive term of this sort rather serves to put us in mind of the particular features of the situation which could have served as reason for the action taken in that very situation. Consider just the list in our case: pride, self-interest, a sense of honor, and fear. For one thing, it is in part false, in part puzzling, to suggest these are motives because they are emotions, or emotions because intelligibly said to have been motives. On the face of it, there is no common element among them by virtue of which they can be regarded as the motives in question in this instance, independently of the 'moving' social prospects facing these men. To take one item, self-interest is not plausibly cast as an emotion. Nor can a sense of honor be identified with the emotions occasionally aroused by its satisfaction or loss. For a different matter, to remind ourselves that episodic fear is a representative passion is not thereby to show that it — the fear, taken supposedly by itself — was a motive for any action.

In the context of explanatory narrative, therefore, such expressions function in a way analogous to individual variables. From the expression, we may (in context) obtain what we believe to be the actual motive involved. What provides for the achievement of understanding is an adequate fund of knowledge concerning the context of the action. Given historical information sufficient for the case, we realize by what events and circumstances men were 'moved' to act as they did. It is significant, for example, that a very substantial account of political and social developments precedes the passage quoted about the secession. For in that account we are shown *what* was taken by these men as an affront to their pride, a threat to their mingled self-interest and sense of honor, and what prospective social changes *constituted* their fear.

II

The Mental-Cause
Theory of Action

Part One

THE PRECEDING CHAPTER was substantially a gloss upon the
observation that a motive is a circumstance because of which
one may take action. That observation was not only explained
but supported. Support consisted both of the exhibition of
standard materials of the sort on which the formulation of fact
was based and of some considerations telling against the received view. In this chapter I shall first indicate the salient differences between that formulation and Gilbert Ryle's familiar
views on motives. Then we shall examine in more detail the
theory behind the conventional doctrine. The last part of
the chapter will show some of the causes and consequences of
adopting that theory.

A good part of the attention Ryle gives the topic of motives
is absorbed in an effort to show that "We must reject . . . the
conclusion . . . that motive words are the names of feelings or

else of tendencies to have feelings." [1] I believe few now would have any quarrel with this claim. However, the positive characterization of motives I gave in the first chapter does noticeably diverge from that given in *The Concept of Mind*. For one thing, I have pointed out, or implied, that motives are happenings and events, among other things. Moreover, since one's motive is the reason one has for a given action, it would do equally to call it "the cause one has for a given action." Yet we have this from Ryle: "Motives are not happenings and are not therefore of the right type to be causes. The expansion of a motive-expression is a law-like sentence and not a report of an event." [2] Having already indicated the point of my agreement with the destructive conclusions of Ryle's analysis of motive-explanations, I shall argue here only the disagreement. Ryle's arguments as to the nature of motives fail to show that motives are dispositions of the agent.

I assume that many readers of *The Concept of Mind* have a stubborn sense that Ryle's presentation of motives as dispositions is somehow completely off target. This suspicion, however inchoate, is correct. The point is a plain one. Whatever in particular one's motive may be, to call it a motive is to think of it as something *by* which one may be moved to act. But an aspect of one's developed character is not as such the sort of thing which moves one.

A disposition *may* afford a motive to the person so disposed. But its doing so is contingent upon a condition independent of its being a disposition. For an illustration, imagine a man such as Tolstoy, struggling to achieve humility. It is an intelligible supposition that such a man might scrupulously avoid situations in which he knew he would be provoked to display

1. *The Concept of Mind* (London, 1949), p. 88.
2. *Ibid.*, p. 113.

those powers of which he was so proud. Then for this man, we could say, a certain disposition was a motive, and was taken by him as motive, to a certain course of conduct. The lesson, of course, is the special feature we have built into the story in order to be able to say this. Unless the judgment is made that his pride should not be gratified, that disposition is not a motive for such an action of restraint or avoidance.

Ryle argues that since (e.g.) vanity is a motive, and to call someone vain is to advert to a complex dispositional property of that person's character, motive-explanations are as such tacit references to such dispositions. I have already indicated that such a statement (that vanity is a certain person's motive) is misunderstood if we ask, in disregard of some given or imagined context, how his vanity explains a particular action. Now we have observed the extraordinary condition to be met for a particular personal disposition to serve the person so disposed as a motive. In addition, it would be well explicitly to note that there are explanations of conduct to which conduct an attributed disposition does not stand as motive, yet for which the disposition is explanatory. Here is a specimen: "Chase did important service; but his uncontrollable vanity and ambition tempted him to mean courses." Certainly "uncontrollable," perhaps also "tempted," militate against our taking this man's vanity and ambition as motives for the conduct in question. Also, the citation of uncontrollable vanity and ambition is at best a meager explanation. Just what we so far lack is any indication of what led, or might reasonably have led, him to do particular things; and so we lack any indication of motives.

Thus motive-explanations do not conform to Ryle's account. Honoring the fact that we do discover the motives of other people, he concludes that "the imputation of a motive for a

particular action is not a causal inference to an unwitnessed
event but the subsumption of an episode proposition under a
law-like proposition." [3] This statement is one of several showing that he mistakes what he in fact achieves for something
else. Ryle gives us a generally acceptable analysis of what is
implicit in the attribution of such traits as greed and vanity to
someone, attributions frequently made as part of an explanation of particular deeds. He mistakes this for an analysis of
how such an attribution typically functions as part of a motive-
explanation.

It is this confusion which leads him to say that "motive
words used [to signify more or less lasting traits in his char-
acter] . . . are elliptical expressions of general hypothetical
propositions of a certain sort, and cannot be construed as expressing categorical narratives of episodes." [4] Ryle's claim is in
jeopardy at the outset, in his taking such words as "vain" and
"indolent" as what he calls "motive words." Rather, to say —
whether expressly or by predicative implication — that someone can be expected to behave in certain ways in certain circumstances can be at most a part of a successful explanation of
his action as proceeding from a certain motive. The part is that
of making it intelligible that such-and-such a circumstance
could have *been* a motive for him. The kind of explanation
needed may be only that of showing that it was not surprising
for this man to take such a circumstance as reason to behave in
such a way. But when one does advert to elements of a man's
formed nature as a way of explaining one or many actions he
did with a certain motive, one is only rarely thereby *stating*
what his motive was. A reading of his character may *make
known* the sort of thing the motive, on particular occasions,

3. *Ibid.,* p. 90.
4. *Ibid.,* p. 85.

was. So again, it is generally false, and only occasionally and contingently true, to say that "a certain motive is a trait in someone's character."[5]

One additional source of Ryle's conviction that motives as such are inclinations or patterns of behavior, is the fact that sometimes to determine just what was the motive on which someone was acting on a given occasion it may be necessary to know him rather well, or subsequently to note his words and deeds over a period of time. Ryle inflates this occasional recourse to a simple standing necessity:

I discover my or your motives in much . . . the same way as I discover my or your abilities. The big practical difference is that I cannot put the subject through his paces in my inquiries into his inclinations as I can in my inquiries into his competences. . . . None the less, ordinary day to day observation normally serves swiftly to settle such questions.[6]

But what one may look to, to determine whether or not some-one in fact acted on a particular motive he had, may be some-thing quite other than the motive itself, for example, that person's knowledge of his own situation at the time of acting.

It should be noted that in passages such as that just given we witness, in effect, a shift in concern away from actual motives to extrinsic cues to their possible adoption by the person in question. This deflection is manifest in Ryle's readiness to talk of determining someone's motives, rather than of deter-mining what (if anything) was the motive of a person in given circumstances for a given action. More significantly, in talking as if a man had to his credit a short inventory of motives — 'had' them all, moreover, over good stretches of time — *The*

5. *Ibid.*, p. 92.
6. *Ibid.*, p. 171.

Concept of Mind surprisingly reflects part of an older picture of motives which Ryle believes he is erasing. That is the would-be literal view of motives as 'springs of action'.

There is a reason, and not mere accident of inattention, for the shortcomings of Ryle's discussion of motives. It is evident in an exclusion he invokes several times but never examines. That is the unqualified contrast of motives and causes. We use some notion of causal efficacy, of one thing's bringing another into being, with regard to diverse kinds of relata: field enclosure and peasant revolt, envy and ulceration, hunger and theft, a protein and the resumption of an enzymatic reaction, forensic skill and the award of damages, a rebuke and a mood, and so on. Part of the program of post-Cartesian thought, however, was the assimilation of causal relations to the transmission of movement by physical contact, so as to eliminate on principle any such pretender as Digby's sympathetic powder. The power, or at least the longevity, of this appeal for reformation is shown even in such assaults upon tradition as Ryle's book. For it is in the course of that very reaction that Ryle relies on the familiar blunt confrontation of 'motive' and 'cause'. He restricts, without explanation, the notion of one thing's being the cause of another.[7]

Perhaps the following remark suggests the explanation Ryle does not himself provide: "To explain an action as done from a specified motive or inclination is not to describe the action as the effect of a specified cause." [8] It is the truth in this observation which leads him then to infer that a motive therefore is simply not a cause. It would seem that Ryle is misled by his awareness of the clumsiness of others with regard to such notions as

7. See pp. 86, 88–89, and especially 113–114.
8. *Ibid.,* p. 113.

those of 'cause' and 'effect'.[9] I take it that what is behind much of Ryle's polemic against construing motives as (episodic) causes is an awareness of the misconception inherent in regarding every action done from a motive as an *effect* of that circumstance. The misconception is one arising from the word itself. Some things which are said to be effects genuinely are made or produced by their causes. It does not follow that every human action for which we could find some kind of true cause is in this sense an effect of that cause. In this regard, then, Ryle's treatment of 'motive' can be seen as a reaction against the view that every human action is, per se, something which is made to happen by antecedent efficient causes.

The older picture of motives whose outline seems to be discernible still behind Ryle's dispositional replacement is that view according to which human actions are limited sequences of psychic process and consequent bodily movement. Call it the mental-cause theory of human action. This is what we shall scrutinize next, as its presence is betrayed in several philosophical works. One recurring modification of this view is worth documenting. That is the thesis that we (ought to) regard the action proper as terminating on the threshold of the physical processes. Richard Price, for example, first proposes that we "conceive that only as, in strict propriety, *done* by a moral agent, which he *intends* to do," then turns this into the still more arresting claim that "our own determinations alone are, most properly, our actions." Clearly this statement invites quite

9. For one brief, admirable complaint against the treatment of "effect," "result," and "consequence" virtually as three titles for one kind of thing, see Empson's paragraph on Fowler's entries in *The Concise Oxford Dictionary* (*The Structure of Complex Words* [London, 1952], pp. 406–7).

different interpretations, given the ambiguity of "determinations." Price goes on to acknowledge this and in such a way as to tip the balance in favor of the internal-process view of 'action': "There are two views of senses, in which we commonly speak of actions. Sometimes we mean by them, the determinations or volitions themselves of a being. . . . And sometimes we mean the real event, or external effect produced." [10]

Part Two

The neglected middle portion of Bentham's *Introduction to the Principles of Morals and Legislation* provides an impressive articulation of mental-cause theory, and of much else as well. In those chapters (VI–XII), Bentham attempts a systematic ordering of such ideas as those of intentionality, motives, dispositions, and actions and their consequences, largely in accordance with that theory. Here it will be enough to note

10. *A Review of the Principal Questions in Morals,* ed. D. D. Raphael (Oxford, 1948), pp. 184, 185. Similarly, consider the main result James achieves in his inquiry into 'volition': "*The essential achievement of the will . . . is to* ATTEND *to a difficult object and hold it fast before the mind.* The so-doing *is* the *fiat;* and it is a mere physiological incident that when the object is thus attended to, immediate motor consequences should ensue" (*The Principles of Psychology,* 2 vols. [New York, 1890], II, 561).

Wittgenstein conceivably had this or similar remarks of James' in mind in imagining the following expression of the sense of discovery to which this view leads: "*Doing* itself seems not to have any volume of experience . . . the phenomenal happenings [seem] only to be consequences of this acting. 'I *do* . . .' seems to have a definite sense, separate from all experience" (*Philosophical Investigations,* trans. G. E. M. Anscombe [Oxford, 1953], p. 161 [Pt. I, para. 620]).

its intrusion even into the ostensibly accommodating sentences at the beginning of his discussion of the nature of motives.

Bentham says this: "By a motive, in the most extensive sense in which the word is ever used with reference to a thinking being, is meant anything that can contribute to give birth to, or even to prevent, any kind of action. Now the action of a thinking being is the act either of the body, or only of the mind." [11] He then goes on to divide 'acts of the mind' in a way which shows — as the notion of a 'thinking being' foreshadows — the clearly Cartesian nature of his pre-emptive convictions. The division is of those mental acts which "rest in the understanding merely" from those which have "influence in the production" of "acts of the will." [12] The first sentence quoted is unexceptionable. We take this use of "to give birth to" to be what it is, figurative. So taken, the statement by itself implies no restriction on what can be a motive. But then immediately we encounter a classificatory interpretation of 'action' which brings in the subordinate notions of an act of the body and an act of the mind. [13]

Is there anything which could be called "an act of the body"? Surely — in the rhetoric of apology or cunning. Or for other extraordinary, rhetorical ends. That is, there is always a special gain being sought when a deed is credited not to oneself but to one's body (or part of it). Consider the boast in Isaiah: "And I looked, and there was none to help; therefore mine own arm brought salvation unto me." Here the isolation of the

11. X.1, para. 2 (*A Fragment on Government and an Introduction to the Principles of Morals and Legislation*, ed. Wilfrid Harrison [Oxford, 1948], p. 214).

12. Compare this with Art. XVIII of Descartes' *Passions*, given below (p. 36).

13. The classification is also Lockean; see, e.g., *An Essay Concerning Human Understanding*, II.9, para. 10, and II.21, para. 4.

speaker is doubly stressed and so his claim to the accomplishment. Of course, the same kind of figure may have a quite different use, as in this line from Housman's parody of a Victorian Sophocles: "A shepherd's questioned mouth informed me that — ." What should arrest us is that synecdoche, and this species in particular, is rightly said to *be* a figure of speech. By "arm," "mouth," etc., we understand something else, the person. The point, with respect to Bentham's maneuver, is that we do *not* seek motives for these acts, when the body or its member (rather than the person) *is* thought of as having done the 'act' in question.[14] For then, in that context, by "act of the body" we mean something which is not (fully, or strictly, or chargeably) the person's doing. If, with Bentham, we were to talk of certain acts of the body as one's own doing, and yet (*per impossible*) were not therein talking figuratively, we should then need to provide for the possibility of their being undertaken for specifiable reasons. To meet this unreal need, only 'acts of the mind' would seem to be available for service as motives for those bodily movements thus (unintelligibly) regarded as actions.

Thus, the mental-cause theory does involve a severe deformation in our concept of a person's acting with, or from, or upon (a) reason. Yet this does not mean that those expressions, notably "springs of action," which are the appointed carriers of the theory, irresistibly deform every narrative in which they occur. For an example to the contrary, here in a remark of Jefferson's (via Henry Adams) is a reliance on such an ex-

14. Consider, for instance, such a report as this: "If unluckily it shall appear and be shown that the panel's *hand* has been the unhappy cause of the death of his brother, . . . at least his heart and purpose have not been in the deed, but his hand only" (from the opening statement in a Scottish murder case of 1795, by defendant's counsel, one David Hume).

pression which we translate, as it were, into a less tendentious account as we read it. The reference is to the American project to buy the Floridas from Spain in 1805: "Not only was it distinctly understood and stated in Mr. Jefferson's own hand at the time that this money 'was to be the exciting motive for France, to whom Spain is in arrears for subsidies,' but in the course of the next week dispatches arrived from Paris containing an informal offer from Talleyrand." [15] We surely are not expected, by the mere presence of "exciting," to be made to suppose that when a man finds himself moved to act he must be suffering Locke's malaise. Rather, I take it that Jefferson's adjective is meant to mark that which the French really held to be good reason to accede to the transfer, or perhaps what was so held by the French as against what had to serve for their Spanish clients.

In general, then, there is no reason to suppose that narrative discourse, even philosophic argument, relying fully on the vocabulary and assumptions of the mental-cause theory can be dismissed out of hand as being perverse throughout. The point of complaint is only that argument so encumbered will show the strain to some extent and at various places. Edwards on 'freedom of the will' is such a case, for example in the discussion of the determination of the will.[16] Note not only the descriptively suspect actors involved — 'the mind', 'the will' — but even more the peculiar stress given by the theory to those verbs designating a motive's 'effect' upon the mind or the will. I mean such as "moves," "excites," "induces," and "invites."

It is perhaps understandable that mental-cause theory, given its radical conceptual alteration of what can be found to be a

15. *John Randolph* (Boston, 1882), p. 164.
16. *Freedom of the Will*, Pt. I, sec. 2, ed. Paul Ramsey (New Haven, 1957), p. 141 f.

person's reasons for acting, should take it for granted that a man's motives (*qua* mental process) are limited to one or several kinds. These kinds, it seems, are limited just by his being a person, or an object in nature. It is not acknowledged that, in practice, decisions as to their identity and number are tied to an account of some specifiable phase of his activity. Predictably, then, the false economy we noted in *The Concept of Mind* is practiced in the confident opening sentences of Bentham's chapter on motives, where he speaks of "the several motives by which human conduct is liable to be influenced."

The resources of the theory have been exploited not only to provide a rationale for penal legislation but also, of course, in the development of psychological theory itself. We shall examine one instance of its deployment in this context. James provides an excellent text for the purpose. He has a statement comparable to Bentham's seemingly open description of a motive as anything giving birth to action. James declares that "objects and thoughts of objects start our action." [17]

This is the opening clause of that section, in his chapter on the will, entitled "Pleasure and Pain as Springs of Action," the single purpose of which is to show that pleasures and pains are

17. *Principles of Psychology*, II, 549. Compare also the position assigned to motives by Kames (Henry Home). The entire passage is worth recording, as a compendium of doctrine: "No man can be conceived to act without some principle leading him to action. All our principles of action resolve into *desires* and *aversions;* for nothing can prompt us to move or exert ourselves in any shape, but what presents some object to be either pursued or avoided. A motive is an object so operating upon the mind, as to produce either desire or aversion" ("Of Liberty and Necessity," in *Essays on the Principles of Morality and Natural Religion* [Edinburgh, 1751], pp. 174–75). I presume he is original in none of this. Certainly his encouraging departure in placing motives outside the mind comes to nothing, since they then become merely the proximate causes of those internal ructions which alone actually 'prompt' us to move.

not the sole springs of action. Taken by itself, James' statement is compatible with what we observed earlier, that all manner of things are our reasons for actions and indeed are so regarded by the individuals who possess these reasons. Further, this cardinal fact might seem to be virtually acknowledged by James, in listing objects separately from thoughts of objects. But only when the statement is taken by itself. For first he turns from a notion which is conveniently general and innocently extensible — that which 'starts' our action — to that of a goad, which is neither: "pleasures and pains are far from being our only stimuli." [18] Then we are given the implicitly exhaustive disjunction of such a stimulus-object's being either sensed or thought of: the objects of our emotions, "whether they be present to our senses, or whether they be merely represented in idea, have this peculiar sort of impulsive power." [19] The same sort of reduction, from a nominally unrestricted universe of motives to objects capable of entering into some mode of 'immediate' contact, recurs in the remainder of the section. For instance, in speaking of "the motives upon which as a matter of fact we *do* act," he describes the "innumerable objects" supplying our motives in such a way as to connect them with us physically: they "innervate our voluntary muscles." [20] In the very course of rejecting simple hedonism for its unwarranted restriction on motives, James pleads that "if the thought of pleasure can impel to action, surely other *thoughts* may." [21]

Finally, having found that "the impelling idea is simply the one which possesses the attention," [22] he turns to the case which looks problematic only in the bad light of theory, namely,

18. *Principles of Psychology,* II, 550.
19. *Ibid.,* II, 550–51.
20. *Ibid.,* II, 552.
21. *Ibid.* (emphasis added).
22. *Ibid.,* II, 559.

negative action; that is, to situations in which one *does* something by not acting, or acts by doing nothing.

> The steadfast occupancy of consciousness . . . [is] the prime condition of impulsive power. It is still more obviously the prime condition of inhibitive power. What checks our impulses is the mere thinking of reasons to the contrary—it is their bare presence to the mind which gives the veto, and makes acts, otherwise seductive, impossible to perform.[23]

All that has preceded this passage shows that James was both serious and consistent in offering the notion of the (would-be literal) presence of reasons to the mind as an equivalent, even an explication, of 'the thinking of reasons'. For "presence to the mind" is apt to achieve in this context the conversion effected throughout by other idiomatic means. Before it was motives, here it is reasons, that are endowed with the potential for physical (and thus genuinely effective) contact. James' 'presence of a reason to the mind' is a recognizable descendant of another concept useful for just such an equivocation, 'an idea'.

There is no sentence here carrying more metaphysical weight than does this one: "The *impulsive quality* of mental states is an attribute behind which we cannot go." [24] Whether it strikes one as oppressively obvious or as the sounding of a deep confusion, the confession makes plain a remarkable difference. Neither in practical life nor in historical narrative is there a general sense of incompleteness to the explanation of actions by the attribution of reasons. There is only diverse and occasional challenge of particular assignments. But with the redemptive effort of mental-cause theory, matters are reversed.

23. *Ibid.*
24. *Ibid.,* II, 551.

This theory, in application, yields dramatically whole actions. The beginning is the adoption of an ideal form of full description, which popular accounts and ordinary history poorly approximate. The middle is the labor at reduction to normal form. The end — and it is a true ending, since we cannot go beyond it — is the apprehension of a mystery.

Part Three

I have drawn attention, by calling it a theory, to the interplay of a certain supposedly empirical ambition with a vocabulary developed to sustain it. To examine this or another theory of human action is to be sensitized to the exploitation of such common expressions as "an action," "taking action," and "a course of action." The effects of past philosophic use are powerful. Consider the calamitous beginning of one modern attempt to state simple truths bearing on the question of Determinism:

You are thirsty, but there is a glass of beer within easy reach; you stretch out your hand, bring the glass to your lips, and drink. Here is what I call a *perfectly clear case* of making something happen. When you brought the glass nearer, that was a perfect instance of what all of us *call* "making something happen." But of course many other simple actions would serve just as well: closing a window, opening a drawer, turning a doorknob, sharpening a pencil. Any number of perfectly clear cases can be found of making something happen.[25]

The last sentence is true, the preceding two false. What could so mislead someone? The fault, I take it, is the unwitting

25. Max Black, "Making Something Happen," in *Models and Metaphors* (Ithaca, 1962), p. 153. Consistently, Black later declares that "when we order somebody to do something, we envisage his making something happen" (p. 166).

adoption of a mental-cause paradigm of human actions. On Cartesian lines one makes a show of analyzing every action (which 'terminates in the body') as if it were one of making something happen. Yet Black unwittingly sponsors, as exemplars of 'making something happen', five bits of human activity which would serve quite nicely to *contrast* with any genuine case of making something happen.

Bringing a glass to one's lips, closing a window, opening a drawer, sharpening a pencil, turning a doorknob: could none of these be an example of making something happen? Of course any one could. Imagine an amputee who is on the verge of mastering his first artificial arm. He carefully visualizes the several muscles about to be called upon and the sequence in which he has been told they must be brought into their unfamiliarly deliberate play, he glares down at his pectoralis, and so on. The moral of the story is that the notion of making something happen is affiliated to that of using an instrumental means to an end.[26]

We might fairly call the error behind the ill-chosen list, The Fallacy of Descartes' Legs. Consider:

Our volitions are of two kinds. One is those actions of the soul which terminate in the soul itself, as when we will to love God, or generally to apply our thought to some object which is not at all material. The other is those actions which terminate in our body, as when solely from having the will to take a walk it follows that our legs move and that we walk.[27]

It could be said of the amputee, after he had become fairly adroit, that from his simply willing to turn a doorknob (in

26. This latter notion is to be understood liberally. The following is an example: "He secured in 1163 a wholesale burning of Cathars at Cologne" (said of a conscientious abbot).

27. *Les passions de l'âme*, Art. XVIII.

reach), it follows that his hand moves and that he turns the doorknob. But not of us. Being what we normally are, a man's body is not, however unavoidably, his instrumentality.

There are now evident and available for consideration two components of the mental-cause theory of human actions. They are, simply, that (1) whenever one (overtly) does something, one makes something happen; and (2) whenever one does something, one makes use of one's body or some part of it to do so.

I noted just now the dependence of 'making something happen' on 'using an instrumental means to an end'. It appears that the reason we exaggerate the scope of (1) is a prior commitment to (2), which involves a special case of 'using an instrumental means to an end'. What is behind (2) is familiar enough. It involves our trying to talk of a person as if he were identifiable as an active being apart from the accident of his body. Here it will be instructive to consider some manifestations of (1) and of (2). The particular cases to be examined may seem to suggest that this complex of ideas had its origin in Cartesian metaphysics. But that would be a false impression. The elements are antique — Platonic, at least, in the case of (2).

The recurrent figure which serves to give expression to (1) and (2) is that of one thing's using another as an instrument. Descartes resorts to this image when he wishes to picture the relation of body to mind in the routine business of waking life: "While united to the body, the mind makes use of it as an instrument to do those sorts of operations with which the mind is usually occupied." [28] Surprisingly, James' thought turns

28. From his sardonic Reply to the Fifth [Gassendi's] Objections to the *Meditations* (ed. and trans. Florence Khodoss [Paris, 1961], p. 229; cf. *Oeuvres*, ed. Charles Adam and Paul Tannery, 12 vols., VII, 354).

out to be very close to that of Descartes, in regard to these fundamental conceptions. At one point, James adopts a description-scheme strikingly like that in Article XVIII of *Les passions de l'âme*. Where Descartes speaks of the simple volition to get up and walk as being followed by the movement of legs, James says, "I will to write, and the act follows." Here is the remark in its own context:

The *willing* terminates with the prevalence of the idea; and whether the act then follows or not is a matter quite immaterial, so far as the willing itself goes. I will to write, and the act follows. I will to sneeze, and it does not. . . . [But] it is as true and good willing as it was when I willed to write. In a word, volition is a psychic or moral fact pure and simple, and is absolutely completed when the stable state of the idea is there.[29]

The passage actually begins with a term of subtle appeal, "prevalence." It echoes the ancient metaphors of agony, the struggle and eventual triumph of reason, will, or appetite. Yet

29. *Principles of Psychology,* II, 560. The omission is this: "I will that the distant table slide over the floor towards me; it also does not. My willing representation can no more instigate my sneezing-centre than it can instigate the table to activity." It is worth noting because here what follows "I will . . ." is such that we do not recognize the description, and because James in effect acknowledges the peculiarity of the description by defending it (in a footnote) with an ineffective and interesting reply: "Only by abstracting from the thought of the impossibility am I able to imagine strongly the table sliding over the floor . . . ," etc.

This will not do. If I have no sense of what it would be for a table to be moved by my 'willing representation' alone, then the description does not belong in a list of instances of willing to do what I might or do conceive to be in my power in that way. The objection can be expressed this way: the referent of "it" in "I will to sneeze . . . ," etc., is the act of sneezing. What act of mine is eligible for the pronoun in "I will that the distant table slide . . . ," etc.?

that is just the conception he also wishes to have us abandon. To James, the prevalence of an idea is nothing more than its 'presence'. In addition, the passage can be taken as a declaration of independence. It may be that, in so thoroughly divorcing the description of the 'motive idea' from that of the 'supervening motion', he means to refuse the fundamental Cartesian distinction among termini of 'acts of the mind'. For on James' account none could 'terminate in' the body.

Still, what matters for us here is the respect in which this remains a Cartesian view. That is, that an active moment in a person's life-history is to be looked upon as consisting of two related events: the volition and the consequent movements of leg and arm, lip and eye. What is important about the two expressions we have just noted of this view is not that, in and of themselves, they are false. For they are not. It is that they are not always — not even often — applicable to those actions Descartes and James take them to fit. In both passages, the presumption is that such a description is normal for the relevant action of walking or writing. It is in this presumption, then, that both are wrong.

There is no need to seek an illustration of this other than in their own words. Each man elsewhere provides a context such that the action *there* mentioned can genuinely be said to follow from the very thought of it. The comparison of the man's remarks will show, in the latter pair of cases, an effective particular addition.

In one letter, Descartes reaches a point where he is concerned to make plain a truth he insists is undeniable by anyone who understands him. That is that only one's thoughts are entirely within one's power; and so, in opposition, that of those functions which belong solely to the body we ought to say "that they are done in the man, and not by the man." To dispel the air of paradox in the first part of this, he glosses *"pensée,"* asking that it be taken

> as I do, for all the soul's operations, . . . not only meditations and volitions, but even the functions of seeing, of hearing, of determining on one movement rather than another, etc., insofar as they depend on [the soul].[30]

What makes the crucial difference here, from Article XVIII of the *Passions,* is "rather than another." For if the context of the account of the action provides certain features, then indeed (e.g.) my legs moving can be taken to follow from the thought or choice that they should do so. These words provide just such a feature, the effective addition in question. They make it possible to interpret the action as genuinely involving choice of the movement. Imagine, say, a crisis when driving, such that two choices confront you, to go left or to go right. It is just some feature which is absent from the perfectly open setting suggested by the corresponding part of Article XVIII, "from having the will to take a walk, it follows that our legs move," etc.[31] It is because of that deficiency that this construction falsely implies that every ('voluntary') movement is the consequence of a determination by the actor *simply* by virtue of being the movement that it happens to be and so no other.

The saving passage in James is one in which he is in the course of arguing for the potency of 'present ideas' alone, without additional and distinctive acts of volition. Here, the words "and, presto! it takes place" might seem to be no more accept-

30. *Oeuvres,* ed. Adam and Tannery, II, 36.

31. There is, of course, the implicative force of "it follows that," and surely it is just this which led Descartes to put the matter as he did. Given this as the only sense in play, the last part of the article ceases to sound grotesque. But it is still false as it stands, for some open (and presumably trivializing) condition about the absence of negativing circumstances must also hold.

able than "and the act follows" in the remark about willing to write and to sneeze. But notice the difference of context:

In all simple and ordinary cases, just as the bare presence of one idea prompts a movement, so the bare presence of another idea will prevent its taking place. Try to feel as if you were crooking your finger, whilst keeping it straight . . . it will not sensibly move, because *its not really moving* is also a part of what you have in mind. Drop *this* idea, think of the movement purely and simply, with all breaks off; and, presto! it takes place with no effort at all.[32]

The difference here lies in the mention of an inhibiting circumstance, now no longer realized, namely, my *keeping* my finger straight. This circumstance corresponds to the other, unrealized movements open to me in the context provided by Descartes' gloss on *"pensée."* In contrast, then, no mention is made in the other James passage — "I will to write, and the act follows," etc. — of negativing conditions, of a proposed or an actual choice among actually presented alternatives.

In another work previously cited, there is further illustration of the necessity of including such an element in accounts of certain actions, if those accounts are to be realistic. Consider the way in which Locke pleads, for the wrong reason, that not doing something may itself properly be called an action.[33] He rightly does not say that (e.g.) not walking or not writing are, perfectly generally, as much actions as are walking and writing. Rather he pictures not walking as an action when there is reason to walk. In short, it is crucial that the action *be* 'proposed'. So Locke speaks of the *forbearance* of an action. The actor does not merely happen not to do the thing in question,

32. *Principles of Psychology,* II, 527. Note the abuse here, amounting to a pun, of "what you have in mind," taken as equivalent for the theoretic expression "the presence of an idea."

33. *Essay,* II.21, para. 28.

he abstains from it. Again, this sense of facing provocation to act otherwise is present in the particular expression chosen for an instance of such forbearance, "holding one's peace."

In a corresponding, and possibly derivative, remark, Bentham also speaks of forbearance.[34] But his remark emphatically endorses the mistaken elements in Locke's, such as the anxious concession that continued use of the vulgar notion is prima facie inconsistent. Having been moved to defend the notion — embarrassing to a mental-cause theorist — of having a motive *not* to do something, he rests everything on Locke's 'determination of the will'. In so doing, Bentham provides a plain instance (all the more astonishing in a mind acquainted with the law) of the view that what any action really is, is a motion.

Locke's attempt to accommodate negative action within his picture shows an equivocation between two distinct views. They concern our identification of episodes in a man's life as actions. One is that the identification turns upon the varied interests of reasonable men (e.g., that an attempt be made to save a human life in sudden peril, conditions permitting). The other, already characterized, is that we consider separately the body and the mind of the actor, looking to see whether movements follow from appropriate thought. It is this assumption Locke betrays by invoking a supposed requirement of determination of the will.[35]

34. X.1, para. 2 (*A Fragment on Government and Introduction to the Principles of Morals,* p. 215 n). Given the bloated sense attached in the mental-cause vocabulary to "voluntary," it is a genuine corruption of the notion of forbearance for Bentham to imply that some forbearances are not 'voluntary'. Indeed, that implication destroys the verisimilitude the notion managed to give the Lockean picture.

35. Interestingly, he later talks of 'voluntary motions' in a passage which culminates in an example — "What causes rest in one [hand], and motion in the other? Nothing but my will, — a thought of my

To suppose that human actions are recognized as such according to this criterion is to try to redescribe them in accordance with (2), the dominant component of mental-cause theory. Accordingly, we may elaborate the difference exhibited by the two pairs of remarks from Descartes and James. In the first member of each pair, there is a phantom element. It is only when circumstances are comparable to those suggested by the second member — Descartes' broad indication of alternative movement, or those concretely described in James' finger-crooking proposal — that action is viewed as following simply from thought. Thus the point of those comparisons is to bring out the role played by our conception of particular circumstance. For it is that which makes it possible in turn to conceive of an immediate sequence of act from thought. But, crucially, the comparison can also serve to explain why the description in Article XVIII has a grotesque aspect. The Cartesian account is an attempt, in accordance with (1) and (2), to have us construe the relation of thought and act as a historic one. Rather, the relation is one of analysis. The necessity of bringing in a certain kind of particular understanding as to circumstance shows that

(a) my arm's moving

follows *from*

(b) my will that it should

only in the timeless sequence of explanatory inference. Determination, in this matter, is found not in the agent's mind but the spectator's comprehension.

---

mind" — very much like James' writing and Descartes' walking. Yet this remark (*Essay,* IV.10, para. 19) is set in a passage which adverts in a general way to conditions that would preclude a person's being able to choose to move his hand. Conceivably, then, the context of Locke's example can be taken to give it at least some of the reality of James' "presto! it takes place."

~~~~~~

———————————— III ————————————

Aberrant Accounts

of What We Do

———————————————————————————————

~~~~~~

Part One

A SAMPLING OF CERTAIN other philosophic observations on human action will provide further witness to the appeal of various aspects of mental-cause theory. In particular, it should be
possible to diagnose some persistent distortions of what it is to
be an unparalyzed, unconstrained individual.

To begin with, here are two remarkable utterances: "No
animal can move immediately anything but the members of
its own body" (Hume); "it is very plain, that when I stir my
finger, it remains passive; but my will which produced the
motion, is active" (Berkeley).[1] The first thing to be said is
that neither of these declarations suffers in being taken from

---

1. *Dialogues Concerning Natural Religion,* Pt. VIII (ed. N. K.
Smith [New York, 1948], p. 186); and *Three Dialogues Between Hylas
and Philonous,* Dialogue II (*The Works of George Berkeley,* 9 vols., ed.
A. A. Luce and T. E. Jessop [London, 1948–1957], II, 217).

its place in dialogue. Each is introduced in its dialogue as an indisputable part of the common understanding, in the light of which certain problematic issues can be better handled. The observation by Hume (here as "Philo") is a leading idea of received philosophical psychology. Yet it is puzzling, because what it entails is comic. It involves our saying that any time a person physically moves something, and not as the result of being himself thrust by another body, he therein moves his own body. But describing a person as acting upon his own body (namely, in moving it) is complementary to describing some part of his body as itself an actor.[2] And so it similarly enjoys a special status, also being special in its uses (e.g., sarcasm).

Once this has been remembered, we see that Philo's statement must be false. So it is. Sometimes we use the poker to move a log on the fire, sometimes we do without it, moving the log with our foot. This reveals the abduction, by mental-cause theory, of the homely distinction between bringing about a certain movement by the use of a given intermediary and doing so without mediation. Theorists commonly talk as if the distinction were fixed by one couple of objects (the actor and his body) between which the relation uniquely holds. The fact, more nearly, is this: we see or do not see a person's moving something as his using an intermediary means to that end, according to what we take to be routine, or anyhow rationally economic, for such an operation. It is in the light of specific practice we believe standard or the obvious choice for the case that we find, or fail to find, the relation to obtain.

Philo's principle has the look of simple truth only if we sup-

2. It is given, of course, that Hume's principle does not concern moving one part of the body with another, as in shifting by hand a leg which is asleep.

press a difference ordinarily recognized. That is the difference exemplified by (a) saying to the amputee in training, "You moved your hand!" in contrast to (b) saying the same thing to a whole person in a variety of imaginable circumstances (e.g., when flirting during prayers, or bidding further at an auction, has been forbidden). It is relevant to grasping this difference that under (b) one may be making *various* kinds of charge. "You moved your hand!" may be said by way of laying a prima facie case against the accused, as it were, final judgment pending. Or it may express the judgment that indeed he did the thing forbidden and express this economically by describing the particular performance on which judgment is based. In circumstances such as those of (a), actor and speaker share a real sense of the actor as an entity distinct from (at least some part of) his body; or, of that part as not a proper member. Neither has this sense when sound of mind and body. Consider this objection: "In describing a man (e.g.) as moving a log not with a poker but with his foot, the very phrase ('with his foot') shows that he did not even then immediately move the log. And so, no animal can move immediately anything but the members of its own body." How should this be answered? By a genuinely rhetorical question: *What* then does his foot mediate, who is the mover its 'employment' keeps from immediate contact with the object moved?

Plainly, what these two remarks have in common — implicit in Philo's declaration, explicit in Hylas' — is the conviction that when a person acts, he makes something happen, inevitably therein acting through the instrumentality of his body. What is necessary is to do more than note that what they say is false. Of course Hylas' statement is a misrepresentation. But not because, say, both the will and the finger are active. The important truth of the matter is that it is not the case that the finger is passive *as against* the activity of something else, the real, unitary agent (self, soul, will, etc.). Similarly with the opening of James' chapter on will, where there occurs a statement of principle culminating in a declaration very much like Hume's: "The only *direct* outward effects of our will are bodily movements." [3] Even more than does Philo's maxim, this formulation invites us to interpret any act of moving a part of one's body as an episode in which the person, in so doing, acts *upon* his body. It is this transformation of our understanding of ourselves as active persons that gives a forced sense, for instance, to James' phrase, "movements which we make." The person is cut off from the body, and every act, with its 'outward effects', is one of making something happen.

This restrictive conception of an action finds expression in a variety of ways, of course. Over-reliance on "produce," as in the following, provides one predictable kind of example: "A cause produces not only its immediate, but also its remote consequences, and the latter no less than the former. I, therefore [in packing up and posting a book], not only produce the immediate movements of parts of my body but also my friend's reception of the book, which results from these." [4] Another

3. *The Principles of Psychology*, 2 vols. (New York, 1890), II, 486.
4. W. D. Ross, *The Right and the Good* (Oxford, 1930), p. 44. Just previously, Ross says this: "An act is the production of a change in the state of affairs. . . . Now the only changes we can *directly* produce are changes in our own bodies, or in our own minds. . . . Consider some comparatively simple act, such as telling the truth or fulfilling a promise. In the first case what I produce directly is movements of my vocal organs" (p. 42). As it happens, he makes this familiar claim in a good cause, that of rebutting certain arguments supplied for a (primitive) utilitarian conception of obligations and duties.

Most relevant aspects of the view expressed in these passages have already been remarked upon, e.g., that (i) a human act is essentially a motion, which (ii) the actor makes happen, by (iii) first making (parts

advocate of this distorted form of that notion, that of bringing something about immediately or directly, even presents it as a "basic limiting principle" of our thought. This is Broad's patient formulation of the undeniable: "We take for granted . . . that a person cannot *directly* initiate or modify by his volition the movement of anything but certain parts of his own body." [5] His particular reason for saying it is to define what he means by "paranormal event," namely any event prima facie contrary to any such principle. Apparently, the exemplary Empiricist concern with psychical research is sustained not simply by mortal hope, or fair play, but by a compulsion to face the inconceivable. I take it this is one factor in James' bringing up for consideration the feat of moving a table by the mere thought of doing so.

We may note an anomaly in mental-cause theory. One manifestation of that complex view is the interpretation of all human actions as episodes of making something happen. Another is the apprehension that there is something innately prob-

---

of) his body move, etc. In addition, Ross' entanglement with 'cause' and its congeners is worth considering. *Do* causes *produce* consequences? Note too the probable change for the better in the next sentence, the choice of "which results from" and not "which is the consequence of."

5. *Lectures on Psychical Research* (New York, 1962), p. 4. Earlier, under the title "Limitations on the Action of Mind on Matter," Broad had located the relation at a prior stage. "It is impossible for an event in a person's mind to produce *directly* any change in the material world except certain changes in his own brain. It is true that it seems to him that many of his volitions produce directly certain movements in his fingers, feet, throat, tongue, etc. These are what he wills, and he knows nothing about the changes in his brain. Nevertheless, it is these brain-changes which are the immediate consequences of his volitions; and the willed movements of his fingers, etc., follow, if they do so, only as rather remote causal descendants" (*Religion, Philosophy and Psychical Research: Selected Essays* [London, 1953], pp. 9–10). But here too he speaks of this as a "basic limiting principle."

lematic in common actions, namely the actual nature (even, the very possibility) of the effective translation of thought into action. Thus it is given out both that a certain form of analytic description is uniquely suitable to human actions, and yet that there is a serious, even irremediable, omission from the protocol.

Sometimes the first of these, the interpretative redescription of simple actions, is only a residual implication, as in Prichard's anxious admission: "I want the iodine to be on my gum. I know that if it is to come to be on my gum, I must *cause it to go* from the end of a brush in my hand to my gum." [6] Sometimes it is avowed, and conscientiously specified. Austin provides a classic example of this: "If I wish to lift the book which is now lying before me, I wish certain movements of my bodily organs, and I employ these as a mean or instrument for the accomplishment of my ultimate end." [7]

This schematic account embodies both elements of mental-cause theory we have discussed. Austin's depiction of favored parts of a person's body as instruments at his disposal is especially worth remarking, for the following reason. The first

6. *Moral Obligation: Essays and Lectures* (Oxford, 1949), p. 185 (emphasis added).

7. *Lectures on Jurisprudence, or the Philosophy of Positive Law,* 3d ed., ed. Robert Campbell (London, 1869), p. 425. This is the context of Austin's careful, or carefully reconstructed, statement: "The wishes which are immediately followed by the bodily movements wished, are the only wishes *immediately followed by their objects.* . . . For example, if I wish that my arm should rise, the desired movement of my arm immediately follows my wish. . . . But if I wish to lift the book . . . [etc.]." Note, again, that it seems appropriate to say that the (allegedly) desired movement of my arm *immediately* follows my wish, only if "my wish" is taken to refer to some occurrent and dynamically effective inner state. Given this supposition, one naturally takes the statement that the desired movement *follows* my wish as a description of a temporal sequence.

part of such an account — "If a man wishes to move an external object, he wishes certain movements of certain parts of his body" — might be construed as necessarily true. As said by a court, for instance, this could be an intelligible and apposite declaration. (That is, provided the case did not make it requisite or prudent to acknowledge the difference between, say, a man's thus 'wishing' to raise his arm and his not simply wishing not to do so.) But the second half of Austin's blueprint ("I employ these as a mean," etc.) forecloses this possibility. Thereby the conditional is presented rather as an elementary causal recipe. This is a result also of his typical use of the notion of that which we immediately bring about. Suppose we were to take the change of location of the book itself as an event segregated by intermediate stages from the person's 'wish' for that outcome. We should then be barred from taking the conditional half of the account as the statement merely of an analytic relation, on the order of "Who wills the end, wills also the means."

As for the seeming realization that we do not (perhaps, can never) see just *how* thought goes over into action, we have already had occasion to remark its candid expression by Locke and by James.[8] Sometimes, however, the confession of metaphysical incapacity is oblique, assigning the inexplicable to some other aspect of activity or awareness. Thus Holmes: "An adult who is master of himself foresees with mysterious ac-

8. Here is one more such, by Russell: "Nothing is less 'intelligible,' in any other sense [than that of 'familiar to imagination'], than the connection between an act of will and its fulfillment" (*Mysticism and Logic, and Other Essays* [London, 1918], pp. 189–90). When he comes to draw the limits of possible human knowledge, Locke makes a counterpart renunciation, concerning the undeniable but inconceivable ability of motion to produce pleasure or pain (*An Essay Concerning Human Understanding,* IV.3, para. 6).

curacy the outward adjustment which will follow his inward effort." [9] Here the sense of mystery is shifted, from our managing to do what in our waking hours we do, to our ability routinely to say what it is we are about to do. The doctrine underlying Holmes' account should, by now, seem unremarkable. Here, as generally, the connection in question has been mistakenly perceived by theorists as temporal, one holding between successive episodes of an individual's life. Thus the fact to be remembered here, as with respect to Descartes' Legs, is *not* that

> (a) the adjustment is not mysterious, but instead partially or completely open to view;

but rather that

> (b) there is normally no such 'adjustment'.

Part Two

Our concern in this chapter and the last part of the preceding has been to see that a historically favored group of notions, centered upon 'making something happen', cannot play the essential role in our comprehension of human action for

---

9. *The Common Law* (Boston, 1881), p. 54. It is worth noting how compactly, in the surrounding remarks, Holmes has used elements of the received theoretical vocabulary: "An act . . . imports intention in a certain sense. It is a muscular contraction, and something more. A spasm is not an act. The contraction of the muscles must be willed. And as an adult who is master of himself foresees with mysterious accuracy the outward adjustment which will follow his inward effort, that adjustment may be said to be intended." I refer not only to the stark picture of an action as a tandem sequence (or concurrence) of inner and outer episodes. There is also the less obviously provocative, and so more effective, image of the normal adult as one who is genuinely obliged to exercise continuous mastery of his body.

which it has been cast. Now we can begin to extend that concern to certain associated misapprehensions about the cardinal notion of human action. To achieve a fitting characterization of 'motive', in Chapter I, it was necessary to set out what it is to *have* a motive. This suggests a comparable procedure with respect to 'action'. Consider the idiom "to *take* action." Here is a full and clear example of its routine use:

The Manichaeans inevitably met with persecution; and their church was too passive, too non-resistant to survive repression. In the end it was stamped out. But the alarm that it had caused was proved by the horror with which the word "Manichaean" came to be regarded. In future the average orthodox Christian, when faced with any sign of dualism, would cry out "Manichaean," and everyone would know that here was rank heresy, and the authorities be seriously disquieted and take action.[10]

The point of reminding oneself how this familiar locution is deployed is to observe more than that it is imbedded in a given context, that is, that an action is *a* thing done. For this fact might look to be an unilluminating, even though necessary, truth — as saying that to take action is always, perforce, to do a particular thing, since actions are particulars. That would fall short of the point, which is this: "to take action" is understood as taking some particular *sort* of action (so, in our example, deprivation, torture, and death). We have already seen that when someone is said *not* to act, or not to take action, he is not being said — as it were, absolutely — to be doing nothing, but rather not to be doing some (understood) thing. It is *that* kind of context to which the notion is bound, one in which we note a type of undertaking. It is not that of being,

10. Steven Runciman, *The Medieval Manichee: A Study of the Christian Dualist Heresy* (Cambridge, 1947), p. 17.

by some criterion (presumably, dateability), a particular thing, a token episode.

This is true not only of the special notion of taking action. The same point can be made about the notion of action itself, as used to meet local, narrative needs. In context, "action" takes its sense from an overt or implicit contrast, as when a historian judges certain persons (in this case, the directors of the East India Company, following Plassey) to have been "bold in exhortation but hesitant of action." Here, what is being regarded as action is nothing less elaborate than the corporate exercise of new authority to meet new responsibilities. As the example may serve to indicate, neither 'action' nor its contrast is fixed for all contexts by some one pair of possibilities — in particular, then, not by the notions of movement and immobility. In this regard, therefore, actions are like motives. Both have suffered theoretical misclassification. Indeed, the mistakes are related: construing an action as a movement of the body, the physical outcome of an effective mental counterpart episode, namely, the motive as 'uneasiness' (and the absence of motive as the non-occurrence of such an internal episode).[11]

11. For an uninhibited post-Lockean view of human action, see the refreshing work of Abraham Tucker [Edward Search], *The Light of Nature Pursued*. Tucker frankly regards actions as motions, e.g., in contrasting "the designs that generate our larger actions" with "the ideas causing our lesser motions" (7th ed., 2 vols. [London, 1848], I, 42–43). His allegiance to theory is firmly stated: "A motive I conceive is the prospect of some end actually in view of the mind at the time of action and urging to attain it: whereas we are apt to take for motives any reasons we can allege in justification of our conduct" (p. 40). It is for *that* reason, accordingly, that "a motive having lost its force is no motive at all" (p. 44). Later on, Tucker discerns active and quiescent states of motives: "Motives, strictly such, are always something actually present in the thought, but they usually retain the name

The doctrine under examination has a persuasiveness which is largely internal to the doctrine itself. That is, the plausibility of various aspects of mental-cause theory is that of apparent implication. Probably the conception of the person as an active being essentially identifiable apart from his (uniquely associated) body has historical priority. Given that persistent conception, it is a natural step to announce as a limiting principle that in overtly doing anything a man makes immediate use of his body, and from that actually to perceiving anything he does as an episode of his making something happen.

Though I believe it would not enter the picture were it not for the existing attraction of this cluster of principles, there is one thing contributing to the powerful appeal of mental-cause theory which can be considered apart from that. This is the economy of some accounts of some human actions. It is a fact that some narratives could (while not otherwise changing character) take a longer form, that of a list of component actions, for instance, of the several stages of a varied and tricky climb, as against the simple statement that the explorer climbed the mountain.

A precaution should be observed here. That complex actions can be factored in this way is not to be confused with the fact that we sometimes redescribe a person's action so as to bring out more definitely how it was he brought about the result mentioned in the initial description. An illustration: initial account, "King Haakon had Snorri Sturluson killed"; redescription, "He ordered that Snorri be strangled." Since this specification procedure is a subject of bad reasoning in both moral philosophy and law, a further remark is needed. Although the procedure can be generally described as 'telling

while remaining in the repository of our ideas, and not directly occurring to view" (p. 144).

54

what he actually did', the redescription is not necessarily more limited in scope than is the initial account (e.g., to movements only). What our illustration shows, of course, is neither that giving the order was only one of a number of component steps the king took in the course of having Snorri killed nor that what Haakon really did was (i) to give an order, *as distinct from* (ii) having Snorri slain. Rather, it is a case of being told that his giving an appropriate order to an appropriate agent *was* his (mode of) securing the poet's death.

To return to complex actions, then, it is their divisibility which allows a partially acceptable interpretation for vague declarations such as that "any act may be correctly described in an indefinite and in principle infinite, number of ways." [12] But even so understood, this statement is at best an abusive exaggeration of fact. What the interpretation leaves to be explained is why one is tempted to make or tolerate such an assertion. One source of this tolerance, I am sure, is that the array of convictions we have examined has as its end product a certain presumption. That is, that a 'voluntary' action is nothing more than a movement of all or part of the actor's body, causally related to certain occurrent inner processes. Given that presumption, it may well further be taken for granted that any discriminable bodily movement within one's natural control is as entitled to be called "an action" as any other.

Tucker obligingly provides an example of an easy slide from plain fact into symptomatic nonsense. From an anecdote with which he opens his chapter on action — one concerning excessively detailed instructions to a servant — he draws the unexceptionable moral that "expedience recommends compendious forms of speech for common use, and puts us often upon

12. Ross, *The Right and the Good*, p. 44.

expressing a long course of action by a single word." But the particular instance of decomposition with which he illustrates this general conclusion proceeds as follows: "We see . . . how many actions are comprised under those three little words, Change the saddles . . . ; lifting up the flap of the saddle, pulling the strap, raising the tongue, drawing out the buckle, taking up the saddle, pulling it towards him, stooping to lay it down, lifting up his body again, and so forth." [13] It is absurd to include the last item, lifting one's body, in this particular inventory. It is a false step if only because of the implicit cross-classification. Each of the others is recognizably a part of the whole operation in virtue of being a distinct member operation upon the equipment involved. Since in raising his trunk the servant operates upon nothing, that moment in the entire episode does not qualify for inclusion in that list. Nor does lifting up his body meet some other criterion (e.g., that of being a movement he had expressly to learn to perform as one item of an ordered repertoire) according to which we should count it as one of the component actions.

Let us ask again, and with regard to Tucker particularly, why the homely category of complex actions is overworked in such a way. Formally the answer would pertain to Tucker's own, obscure, proposal to "call one action so much as passes between each perception and the next." [14] But since he does

13. Tucker, *The Light of Nature Pursued*, I, 22.

14. In one of his most Shandean passages, he tells us just previously exactly what transpires during such intervals: "How nimble are the motions of the fencer and the tennis player! . . . [Yet] between every impulse of the object and every motion of the hand, an entire perception and volition must intervene. How readily do our words occur to us in discourse, and as readily find utterance at the tongue the moment they present themselves! The tongue . . . receives every motion and forms every modulation of voice by particular direction from the mind. Objects and ideas rise continually in view. . . . Yet volition keeps pace

not at all conceive of this as an arbitrary, let alone miscon-
ceived, proposal, our question concerns rather what underlies
the adoption of any such criterion for the identity of an action.
The supporting argument for a position like Tucker's, though
usually tacit, seems to be something like the following. Real
causes are thrusts, contact forces impelling or arresting movement. For human movements there are two unproblematic
kinds of cause. There are those which are plainly and completely external, such as the jogging of one's arm; and, as
plainly, those which are mediated by the body alone, such as
a very painful stimulus to withdrawal. But we recognize also
a third kind, to account for the rest of one's actions — that is,
those done of one's own agency. For these, "voluntary" is said
to be suitable as a synoptic title. So, those parts of a complex
action that are not held to proceed from causes of the previous
two kinds are to be credited by default to the third, to mental
forces somehow inducing appropriate bodily processes.

This conception of "voluntary" as of very general application,
and as a name for some common positive feature of a great
many actions, is at work in unlikely places. I believe it lies behind Ross' surprisingly easy dismissal of Aristotle's distinction,
among agents who by reason of ignorance do a harmful act,
of the involuntary from the merely nonvoluntary, according
as the agent is or is not pained at what he has done.[15] This
is Ross' comment: "This distinction is not satisfactory. There

---

with perception and sometimes perhaps out-strips it: for in speaking
the word MIND the whole idea seems to present in one perception,
but there must be four several volitions to guide the tongue successively
in pronouncing the four different letters" (*ibid.*, I, 23).

In his *Dictionary of National Biography* piece on Tucker, Leslie
Stephen nicely observed that "his psychological and ethical remarks
. . . are full of interest."

15. *Nicomachean Ethics* III.1 (at 1110^b18 ff.).

is no real difference of meaning between 'involuntary' and 'non-voluntary'. . . . it is clear that unwilling and merely involuntary acts cannot be differentiated by the agent's subsequent attitude." [16] But there is a real ground of difference, if pitiableness is a criterion of the involuntary. It is incriminating, then, for an admirer of Aristotle to attach "merely" to "involuntary."

Now, our reconstructed sketch of Volition's putative role contains a natural index of simplicity, since therein each self-controlled change of direction requires a peculiar thrust. A (so-called) voluntary action will be taken to be complex if, and at least to the extent that, it consists of movements of a patient member of the body in more than one direction. Raising up one's trunk is more than barely admissible to the list of actions involved in changing saddles. It is far more nearly an atomic action than is even such an undemanding step as unbuckling a strap. [17]

I have now indicated how fixation on contact force as true cause may account for such a conviction as Tucker expresses in declaring that "all our performances and transactions are made up of momentary acts." [18] An essential part is played also by the unrealistically uniform distinction of the actor from the bodily medium of execution. Tucker, of course, does not

16. *Aristotle,* 5th ed. (London, 1949), p. 198.

17. Though, in the excitement of theory, even this fantasy of one motion/one volition may seem an incomplete deduction: "When upon finding yourself thirsty in a sultry day you snatch up a cup of liquor, if after you have gotten it half way up, you espy a wasp floating on the surface, you thrust it instantly from you; which shows that one volition is not sufficient to lift your hand to your mouth, for you see the mind may take a contrary turn in that little interval" (Tucker, *The Light of Nature Pursued,* I, 23).

18. *Ibid.,* I, 24.

fail to make this extended distinction. Even when pressing to extravagance the theory he has received, he is usually careful to identify the actor by its generically proper name, "the mind." He not only enumerates the possible 'actions of the mind' (in his view, two only), but finds that what *we* do strictly is confined to such actions. He speaks (e.g.) of the action of the mind as being our own proper action, having earlier sided with Locke in finding no other agent in the mind but the mind itself.[19] Seen against the work of one of his descendants, Locke's inconsistency on this matter is a virtue. His actual choice of expression registers the strain of employing the language of theory.[20]

19. *Ibid.,* I, 33, 21.
20. In one paragraph, for instance, Locke moves from identifying the mind as the actor, to the person, and back to the mind. (*Essay,* II.21, para. 30.)

—————————— IV ——————————

'Motivation' and 'Behavior'

as Temptations

Part One

THROUGHOUT THE PRECEDING CHAPTERS I have been arguing principally for two connected points. They are that motives and actions are more various in kind than is commonly allowed in philosophical writing on the subject; and that motives (and, by implication, intentions and purposes as well) are taken as accounting for those episodes of conduct which they do explain in ways not to be assimilated to the physical model of contact force. In that light we have inspected a number of severe misrepresentations of everyday life. The connecting thread among them is their authors' submission to an uncalled-for theory. This provides at least a gross explanation of an evident hunger to systematize our common appreciation of 'voluntary' actions, and to do so by imposing artifice upon the facts.

I take for granted that simple critical inertia cannot be the sole reason such pretensions continue to appeal to good minds. A reason so far not explicitly considered is this. Certain views on the relation of thought to action are dominated by the consideration that, for human activities as for any other natural event, cause precedes effect. We have already anticipated a kind of persuasive maneuver based on this abstract principle. It goes as follows. Given that distinctly human acts seem to arise neither from externally impressed forces nor from anything within our bodies comparably sufficient and simple, we are to postulate (even, admit reflective intimacy with) generative mental acts.

Yet even if accepted, this claim is not enough to establish mental-cause theory. The principle that all human acts, not excluding those fully chargeable to the actor, have causes and that these causes must be precedent to those acts wants interpretation. That has been supplied by incorporating within the received philosophical vocabulary the presumption that such causes, even if immaterial, essentially mimic the primitive experience of pushing and being pushed. Here (and from a tradition other than that of British Empiricism) is one such global interpretation, candid and fantastic: "The feeling of responsibility assumes that I acted freely, *that my own desires impelled me* [dass mein eigner Wunsch die Triebfeder war]." [1]

1. Moritz Schlick, *Fragen der Ethik* (Vienna, 1930), p. 114 (*Problems of Ethics,* trans. David Rynin [New York, 1939], p. 155; emphasis added). In the light of this, it seems fair to take a remark Schlick makes just before as also expressive of his uncritical belief in the existence of some one positive, though variously nameable, characteristic essential to genuine action. This is the earlier remark: "What is this consciousness of having been the true doer of the act, the actual instigator? Evidently not merely that it was he who took the steps required for its performance; but there must be added the awareness that he did it 'independently,' 'of his own initiative,' *or however it be expressed*" (*ibid.,* p. 154; emphasis added).

Undeniably, it is the universal experience of contact and displacement which gives initial life to such indispensable notions as those of a man's being driven, or led, or compelled, or inclined, or blocked by (his appreciation of) the pressing facts. But philosophers have, in effect, become literalists in these matters. I believe it is only the influence of some such concealed rule for interpretation as that just sketched which can explain Schlick's acceptance of a daemonic representation of human action and accountability. And that in a book in which "the subject-matter for consideration" is propositions "such as occur in daily life (for example, 'This man is well-intentioned'; 'That man was completely responsible for his act')." [2]

These assumptions also seem often to underlie the employment, in philosophical quarrels, of familiar terms taken from the current vocabulary of psychology and the social sciences. We shall examine just one case of such borrowing. A well-known critique of the logic of explanation contains an incidental attack on the proposal that explanations (e.g.) in diplomatic history are typically different in important respects from those accepted (e.g.) in mechanics. Specifically, Hempel and Oppenheim confront the view that since "the explanation of any phenomenon involving purposive behavior calls for reference to motivations," "the causal type of explanation is essentially inadequate . . . in the study of purposive behavior." [3] The durable controversy they enter has in the past been

2. *Ibid.*, p. xiv.

3. "The Logic of Explanation," *Philosophy of Science*, Vol. 15 (1948), pp. 135-75; reprinted in *Readings in the Philosophy of Science*, ed. Herbert Feigl and May Brodbeck (New York, 1953), pp. 319-52. Citations will be of the slightly abbreviated version in the Feigl and Brodbeck collection, here pp. 326, 327. The essay is also available in Hempel's collection, *Aspects of Scientific Explanation, and Other Essays in the Philosophy of Science* (New York, 1965).

fed by unclear or partisan apprehensions of the genuine problems involved. This attempt by Hempel and Oppenheim to finish off the dispute is likewise faulty in the very ways they formulate the issue. Their choice of descriptions is already *ex parte*. As for their argument, the remarkable aspect of it is the confidence with which they rely on the sort of assumption (Always Push, Never Pull) under discussion here. It will be useful to have the full argument for examination.

Unquestionably, many of the — frequently incomplete — explanations which are offered for human actions involve reference to goals and motives; but does this make them essentially different from the causal explanations of physics and chemistry? One difference which suggests itself lies in the circumstance that in motivated behavior, the future appears to affect the present in a manner which is not found in the causal explanations of the physical sciences. But clearly, when the action of a person is motivated, say, by the desire to reach a certain objective, then it is not the as yet unrealized future event of attaining that goal which can be said to determine his present behavior, for indeed the goal may never be actually reached; rather — to put it in crude terms — it is (a) his desire, present before the action, to attain that particular objective, and (b) his belief, likewise present before the action, that such and such a course of action is most likely to have the desired effect. The determining motives and beliefs, therefore, have to be classified among the antecedent conditions of a motivational explanation, and there is no formal difference on this account between motivational and causal explanation.[4]

But clearly, for persons, some as yet unrealized attainment often does determine their behavior. Hempel and Oppenheim present us with that commonplace, paradox taken as embarrassingly plain truth.

Several parts of this passage need to be considered, those

4. Feigl and Brodbeck, *Readings,* pp. 327–28.

trading on such notions as 'behavior', 'motivation', and 'a course of action'. In effect, they are used to discount any appeal ostensibly to a future state of affairs for explanation of an action. They make it out to be an explanation which really adverts (at least implicitly) to a present state, here said to be a combination of desire and belief. That it *is* an interpretation — whether warranted or not — is evident just in the shift from talking of goals and of the future (first and second sentences) to speaking of a *desire* to reach a certain objective (third sentence). Our aim, then, is primarily that of seeing how this shift is made plausible. My proposal is that certain of the operative words and phrases in this passage are theory-partial. It is to that aspect of the passage that we shall turn our attention. It should be understood that there is nothing idiosyncratic in their way of framing matters. The viewpoint Hempel and Oppenheim express, if not the terms they deploy, can readily be found in philosophical work otherwise of a quite different character.[5]

Consideration should start with their use of "behavior," which may well produce confusion, since it helps maintain a certain illusion. That is, that by some one word or phrase we can refer informatively to anything a given kind of subject — say, men — may do. Consider a difference, then, with regard to the verb. When we tell someone to behave, we are understood (if at all) as telling him to do certain sorts of things, or to do them in an understood manner. For given persons and

5. As in the following (*n.b.* "of course"): "The expression 'determined to act for one's own pleasure' is in itself seriously misleading. Even when we are acting with a direct view to our own future pleasure, it is, of course, the *present* pleasure attaching to the idea of our future pleasure, not the future pleasure itself, which determines our action" (Ernest Albee, *A History of English Utilitarianism* [London, 1902], p. 98, n. 2).

places, the understanding may be very liberal, perhaps just that he is to put *some* limit on folly or indifference or libido. Yet the notion *is* tied, in genuine use, to some determined area of application. Telling someone that he has behaved, or has behaved well, is connected with what you take his role or aspirations to be — that of a boy, a knight, a novice, a dog.

Accordingly, this standard dictionary entry is economic and accurate: "*behave,* to conduct oneself in a specified way." Note, not "to conduct oneself," *simpliciter*. The addition is inevitable. There is no absolute sense in which a man leads or carries himself, has or takes control of himself. He does so with respect to discrete opportunities for excess, betrayal, trespass, or fugue.

Similarly with the substantive. Even in its most general sense (significantly, recognized by the *Oxford English Dictionary* as a transferred sense) it remains "the manner in which a thing acts under *specified* conditions or circumstances, or in relation to other things." [6] The transfer is from (i) a sense related to general notions of facets of human life in a civil society ("Manner of conducting oneself in the external relations of life") to (ii) a sense applicable to limited aspects of the 'life' histories of subjects other than human beings. The transfer is not in the other direction. The notion of behavior does not apparently have a source in a perfectly general sense of change of state or place, under which characteristically human undertakings are to be subsumed by virtue of their participation in this one comprehensive nature.

As for the other parent of 'motivated behavior', part of what I have to say about 'motivation' is surmise. It seems that frequently it is presumed to be public knowledge by now that a group of popular conceptions, such as those of 'intention' and 'reason', somehow fails to capture our general sense of what is

6. Emphasis added.

typically involved in human actions. Perhaps the unspoken grievance is that such conceptions are not genuinely discriminable from one another within vulgar discourse, or that they are inherently imprecise or anachronistically specialized. Honoring some such presumption, one may turn to "motivation" for release from this poverty. The good news, it may seem, is that here finally is a term standing for the very type of that which really moves a person to act, when he is acting accountably — that is, for all (or always enough) of a set of such things as desire, deliberation, and decisive choice.[7]

Certainly "motivation" has the advantage of youth. The word came into the language only recently (approximately a century ago) and, it seems likely, as the carrier of the theoretic burden just indicated. It is probable that Schopenhauer is the immediate source of the notion. Consider his declaration that motivation is causality seen from within.[8] This follows upon his speaking of our having, with respect to actions whose causes are motives, an insight into the inner aspect of the (*sic*) process of causation. Not surprisingly, Leibniz thus appears to have been a prime mover in this development. One relevant part of his work is the expansion he proposes for Locke's "great motive," transforming that uneasiness into *petites impulsions* which are both unfelt and uninterrupted.[9] Further,

7. To save from misunderstanding: nothing here is meant to imply a general assessment of the established vocabulary peculiar to an area, say, of experimental psychology, not even talk of continuously acting motivations. This part of the chapter bears only on the indiscriminate detachment of such expressions for service elsewhere.

8. *The Fourfold Root of the Principle of Sufficient Reason*, sec. 43.

9. This is Leibniz' comment (on Locke's *Essay*, II.21, para. 29):

If you take your *uneasiness* or *inquietude* as a veritable displeasure, in this sense I do not admit that it is the sole incentive [*aiguillon*]. Most frequently these are the little insensible perceptions which might be called imperceptible pains if the notion of *pain* did not

it is reasonable to suppose that the domestication of 'motivation' largely accounts for what (to my knowledge) has not received explanation and so stands, implausibly, as a historical accident. I mean the extinction of 'springs of action'. James is a significant transition figure, in this regard. He uses both notions in *The Principles of Psychology,* and apparently interchangeably.[10]

The acceptance of the term so soon after its introduction shows that it filled *some* presumed deficiency. One likely attraction of "motivation" (even over "motive") is that its use can have the air of invoking a truly coherent, because continuous, inner 'causal' process.[11] Inventive theoreticians had previously talked as if a Plenum of Volitions (again, when one is acting 'voluntarily') were a known, even a necessary, truth.

---

include *apperception.* These little impulsions consist in delivering themselves continually from little obstacles towards which our nature works without thinking of them. This *uneasiness* consists in truth in this, that we feel without knowing it, which fact makes us act in passion as well as when we appear most tranquil; for we are never without some action and motion, which arises only from the fact that nature always labors to put herself more at her ease" (*New Essays Concerning Human Understanding,* trans. A. G. Langley [LaSalle, 1949], p. 194).

10. I cannot say whether he is particularly indebted for "motivation" to Schopenhauer. Perry does observe that "In the early '70s . . . James read Schopenhauer's *Fourfold Root of the Principle of Sufficient Reason,* with special reference to what is and is not given in immediate conscious perception" (R. B. Perry, *The Thought and Character of William James,* 2 vols. [Boston, 1935], I, 721).

11. Another, that it may have seemed to acknowledge and name a missing helpmeet for the notion of association; namely, an unfailing process making intelligible not only our wittingly guided actions but all the large remainder for which no *ad hoc* executive thought is detectable. Thus the twin couplings of idea with idea and of thought with deed could more confidently be taken as steadfast complement, for the inner life, of the materially ubiquitous discipline of gravitation.

Thus Mill: "Have we, when we have finished reading a volume, the smallest memory of our successive volitions to turn the pages? On the contrary, we only know that we must have turned them, because, without doing so, we could not have read to the end. Yet these volitions were not latent: every time we turned over a leaf, we must have formed a conscious purpose of turning; but . . . [we have no] more than momentary remembrance of it." This is from the chapter in which Mill arrives at a highly qualified acceptance of the doctrine of 'unconscious mental modifications'.[12] Its interest for us here is in making plain that the Plenum of Volitions is called up to account for even routine 'voluntary' actions. Consider, in particular, "every time we turned over a leaf, we *must have* formed a conscious purpose of turning." In context, this inference to an inner causal process is taken as parallel to the other one, "we *must have* turned them." That is, as an inference to a specific kind of event, a deduction based upon what are implicitly taken by Mill as parallel general principles. Those principles would be expressed in something like the following formulas: "If the pages are not turned, they cannot be read," as a model for "If one has no volition to (move the hand to) turn the page, one('s hand) does not turn the page." It can be shown that this is another view not unique to British Empiricism. Here is Bosanquet: "Almost all our waking life is carried on by actions such as walking and sitting, which we hardly know that we will, but which we could not do if we did not will them." [13]

12. *An Examination of Sir William Hamilton's Philosophy and of the Principal Philosophical Questions Discussed in his Writings*, 2 vols. in one (New York, 1884), II, 17. See especially pp. 21–24, following Mill's ironic conceit about Hamilton's inability to remember his own thoughts.

13. *The Essentials of Logic, Being Ten Lectures on Judgment and*

If this report of the rationale and force of 'motivation' is at all accurate, then we have in hand at least some explanation of Hempel and Oppenheim's failure to discriminate among explanations referring variously (e.g.) to intentions, motives, or purposes. For that is the peculiarity of the notion of 'motivated behavior' as it is invoked in their statement. It is apparently supposed to be the notion of that essence of full human action with which we are all, or can easily be taught to become, familiar. Hence, the use of the omnibus expression "motivated behavior," at least in such a context, is symptomatic of a false conception of human doings.[14] For it is natural to take this hybrid notion as a reflection of a truly counterpart mode of association in a person's life. The very notion can help induce us to look upon most coherent moments of our active lives as an effective joining of certain inner experiences (taken, e.g., as intentions) to certain outer experiences (usually regarded as actions proper), i.e., behavior.

Accordingly, speaking of the *action* of a person as that which is the locus of 'motivation' can well be a manifestation of the

---

Inference (London, 1895), p. 39. The reasoning underlying faith in the Plenum of Volitions is a little more explicitly revealed in a preceding passage: "When . . . one stands looking at a picture, one's immediate conscious purpose is to study the picture. One also entertains dimly or by force of habit the purpose to remain standing, which is a curious though common instance of will. We do not attend to the purpose of walking or standing, yet we only walk or stand (in normal conditions of mind) as long as we will to do so. If we go to sleep or faint, we shall fall down" (p. 38). Then he flatly declares that "whenever we are awake we are willing" (p. 40).

14. It will be apparent now that considerations of style do not stand behind my choosing this variety of expressions, some of them awkward. I mean such as "action(s)," "activities," "conduct," "attainment," "undertaking(s)," "doings," "achievement(s)," etc. It might have been thought that some one of them could perfectly well do for all. None can, perfectly well.

same surreptitious program. Again I am speaking only of a likelihood. We do often enough speak of an action as having had a certain motive, and in no way suggest any restrictions of the kind in question here. But in Hempel and Oppenheim's argument, these words do become problematic. They are an invitation to regard actions, *as against* persons, as the sort of thing that can strictly be said to have a motive (i.e., be 'motivated').

The remarks Hempel and Oppenheim next make are interesting in being concerned with a phantom problem, one whose appearance of reality is a projection of a mistake parenthetically urged upon us in the opening sentence: "Neither does the fact that motives are not accessible to direct observation by an outside observer constitute an essential difference between the two kinds of explanation; for also the determining factors adduced in physical explanations are very frequently inaccessible to direct observation. . . . Similarly, the presence of certain motivations may be ascertainable only by indirect methods, which may include reference to linguistic utterances of the person in question, slips of the pen or of the tongue, etc." [15] Whether this claim — that motives are not accessible to direct observation by an outside observer — is taken as true or false depends upon the password "observation." A first response is to say that of course the motives of one man are accessible to observation by another, given sufficient play with the notion of 'observation'. (The reason above all why one wants to be able to say something like this is that according to the view which Hempel and Oppenheim here represent the motives of another person, if not also one's own, are always known only inferentially.) Under this dispensation, for example, my reading a particular document attesting to a cer-

15. "The Logic of Explanation," p. 328.

tain secret marriage, my performance of one or more comparative and material tests to rule against routine possibilities of forgery, predating, and interpolation, and perhaps further reading to confirm that the Thomas Cranmer cited was indeed the archbishop, would count as the exploitation of access to 'observation' of his motive for one or more acts in his life. ("Direct" would seem not false but out of place here.)

More agreeably, we should concede that the motives of another are inaccessible to direct observation, indeed necessarily so. That is, when anything definite is meant by "observation." The reason for this is different from what Hempel and Oppenheim imagine. It is that motives are not accessible to just any observation. (Or, that they are not accessible as motives *just* to observation.) Hempel and Oppenheim have, as it were, mistaken the kind of necessity which accounts for this. For it is not that the peculiar constitution of intelligent bodies is such that their motives and intentions are screened from outer observation. Rather, we see (i.e., realize) *that* such-and-such is or was or might be motive for so-and-so to do a certain thing. For plausible use, this somewhat contrived notion of 'observing someone's motive' depends upon an anterior acceptance of the motive, any motive, as an object. One's motive for a certain action may, of course, quite literally be an object standing out in one's view. But as motive it is present or available to one's attention in a particular light. That is, as giving reason, in the circumstances, for a certain (type of) action.

It is significant that Hempel and Oppenheim shift from "the fact that *motives* are not accessible" to "the presence of certain *motivations* may be ascertainable." This substitution serves to accommodate the assignment of sheer presence to desires, beliefs, and motives. The very notion of 'the presence of a motivation' is a puzzling one, given that "motivation" is supposed to be an innocent (or, superior) replacement for "motive." That the authors should couple 'the presence of a motivation' to 'the presence of an electric charge' is an indication of what kind of theoretic investment has been made in 'motivation'. The vocabulary of their argument works to win acceptance for the attachment of intrinsic 'presence' to a motive. Specifically, the covert force of "motivation" is required, the sense of internal process tending to visible action (i.e., 'behavior') as its occasional result. The substitution of "motivation" for "motive" thus prepares the way for the novel conception in an obvious respect. Token processes are intrinsically located in both duration and place. Quite ordinary motives may not be — for example, an opportunity, such as potential access to new markets, or a social role, such as the status of being married.

In sum, the shift is a rhetorical provision. It prepares us to regard motives and intentions as entities generically limited to a kind of place (beneath the skin), and as essentially fixed in time (not later than the associated behavior); that is, as having a total *kind* of presence. In turn, associating "presence" in this way with "motivation" is not openly provocative as it would be with "motive." Thus in this notion of the presence of motivation, each insecure element supports the other.

Part Two

I have suggested that philosophical uses of certain familiar notions, notably 'behavior' and 'motivation', are suspect. There is a likelihood, in contexts in which anything problematic turns upon their use, that we may unwittingly be committed by their use to the acceptance of distorted representations of ourselves. Similarly, although the notion of what determines someone's behavior has applications that are free of theoretic preconception, it too can be abused. It is abused in the argument constructed by Hempel and Oppenheim. There is an inhibition manifest in saying that it is desires and beliefs present *before* the action that determine one's behavior, for those occasions when we explain a piece of behavior by invoking a motive. This is a restriction on the notion of that which could possibly determine what one does, such that it is taken as standing for one kind of cause. The result is that *whatever* is said to determine (on a given occasion) what one does, can *only* be antecedent to one's activity. A further result of such an inhibition is that we are again offered a reductive analysis of motive-explanations, and in terms which beg the question of the adequacy of that analysis. In sum, a generalized notion of 'behavior' obscures matters by covering with metaphor the prima facie differences at issue, such as that between saying a man's irritable behavior was determined by (or, was a response to) his hypoglycemic condition and saying, of an anthropologist, that his seemingly incurious behavior was determined by his conviction (or, was a response to his being advised) that this would insure his quick acceptance by the tribe.

It might be said, of so wide an employment of the notion of that which determines a man's behavior, that some such ample use is implicitly justified by the fact that we commonly accept a plurality of accounts of a single transaction — that we can sometimes give both ground and causes proper for a man's action, and so may justifiably use "determining conditions" as the family name, and correspondingly use "behavior" as the common title of his action and his (mere) movements. This defense does not seem workable, however, since what it adduces as fact is not in evidence when cases are examined. In particular, the facts do not support the claim that radically different kinds of 'determining condition', each sufficient in itself, can be cited to account for the very same episodes in one's life. At least, that is my judgment on some contemporary instances of such a claim. We shall briefly consider three similar specimens.

There is a passage in Ryle's well-known dismissal of the Bogy of Mechanism in which he rejects the assumption that "there is some contradiction in saying that one and the same occurrence is governed both by mechanical laws and by moral principles, an assumption as baseless as the assumption that a golfer cannot at once conform to the laws of ballistics *and* obey the rules of golf *and* play with elegance and skill." [16] Whatever one's verdict on the fears expressed by some philosophers, it must be said that this example simply does not show that the assumption on which those fears allegedly rest is baseless. The inadequacy is not in a lack of correspondence between the two assumptions, but in the infirmity of Ryle's ground for claiming that the second one is baseless. None of the pairings among (1) that which conforms to the laws of ballistics, (2) what constitutes the golfer's obedience to the rules of the game, and (3) that wherein he displays his skill is a matching of (different descriptions of) one and the same thing. That which conforms to the laws of ballistics is (1′) the ball, or the flights of the ball, whereas what constitutes (or manifests) obedience to the rules of the game is (2′) certain sequences of the player's acts and choices, and he exercises his skill in (3′) such matters as the planning and execution of his shots.[17]

16. *The Concept of Mind* (London, 1949), pp. 80–81.
17. Much of the same may be said of this: "It is by no means a clearly correct assumption that explanation of an event in terms of an agent's decision must exclude the possibility of giving a causal explanation of it as well. In order to maintain that the occupant of the next room *decided* to turn on the lights it is not necessary, nor indeed is it possible, to deny that their lighting up was an ordinary instance of the

There is a more nearly persuasive passage in *The Concept of Mind*. It comes after Ryle's parable of the chess spectator who, ignorant of what it is to be a player in a game and seeing at first only the actual, rule-governed changes of position on the board, foolishly declares that "heartless necessity dictates the play, leaving no room in it for intelligence or purpose." Ryle says that "what the illustration is meant to bring out is the fact there is no contradiction in saying that one and the same process, such as the move of a bishop, is in accordance with two principles of completely different types." [18] But note how he purports to reveal to us *one* thing which is both obedient to the rules of the game and in conformity with some tactical principle:

A spectator might ask, in one sense of "why," why the bishop always ends a move on a square of the same colour as that on which it began the game; he would be answered by being referred to the rules of chess, including those prescribing the design of the

laws of electricity. And to say that the golf-ball finished short of the green because the player wanted to keep out of the bunkers does not make it either incorrect or impossible to explain its flight in terms of the elasticity of ball and club-face, the velocity of impact, and the state of atmosphere and ground" (G. J. Warnock, " 'Every event has a cause'," in *Logic and Language,* 2d Series, ed. A. G. N. Flew [Oxford, 1953], p. 96). Two comments are enough. The lighting-up case shows nothing, since Warnock begins by speaking of *an* event, but then speaks of two, the throwing of the switch and the coming into operation of the circuit. That is, to get rid of the illusion that these are explanations of the same thing, notice that mention of one thing (the decision) is a way of indicating that an initial condition of the other (the functioning of the circuit) has been met, in a particular way. As for the golf case, giving information about what the player wanted is tantamount to answering a question about why he hit the ball as he did, and so is *not* an answer to a question about why, given a certain impact, the ball then had a certain flight and roll.

18. Pp. 77, 78.

board. He might then ask, in another sense of "why," why a player at a certain stage of the game moved one of his bishops (and not some other piece) to one square (and not to another); he might be answered that it was to force the opposing Queen to cease to threaten the player's King.[19]

Again, a steady look at the exemplary case fails to reveal the convergence of different principles of explanation on one subject.[20] Here it fails likewise to discover the imputed duplicity of "why?" The first question the spectator is here represented as asking is why the (*type* of piece known as the) bishop is (always) moved in a certain *kind* of way. The second question, in contrast, asks why a (particular) piece in a particular situation was moved to an individually identified square.

The same difference — the absence of 'one and the same process' — can be brought out by the following considerations. It may be tempting to suppose that in Ryle's story the set of actual moves constitutes the one subject the nature of which is due, simultaneously, to different determining conditions (namely, constitutive rules and tactical principles), and similarly for the actual motions of the ball in the golf stories. Yet this is not so. It is not just that the rules of the game fail es-

19. P. 78.

20. The same problem, that of even finding the allegedly identical subject of radically different kinds of determining condition, is emphatically presented by Kant's talk of freedom and natural necessity in the same human actions [*ebenderselben menschlichen Handlungen*]. His dominant view is not what it is sometimes reported as being, that one of a pair of somehow correlated subjects is genuinely free and creative, the other mechanically determined. Rather, in Beck's paraphrase, it is the economic and striking belief that "every event in human conduct can be seen . . . in two ways: as a necessary consequence of preceding events and as directly determined by the intelligible character" (L. W. Beck, *A Commentary on Kant's Critique of Practical Reason* [Chicago, 1960], p. 191).

sentially to determine specific moves. Rather, an actual move, the episode itself, is *neither* obedience to a rule of the game nor conformity to a tactical principle. What is an instance, for chess, of such obedience is, roughly, (a) moving that (kind of) piece, when one is playing, to that (kind of) square. What is an instance of such conformity is (b) moving that piece in that (optional) way *in that situation*. The identical change of position of the object could be done, say, with only one piece on the board, and with a purely decorative purpose and effect, that of more nearly centering the solitary object on its ground.

A last observation to be made about Hempel and Oppenheim's argument concerns their recourse at one point to the notion of a *course* of action. They say that one component of any 'motivation' is a "belief, . . . present before the action, that such and such a course of action is most likely to have the desired effect." The passages we have examined from their paper tend to effect a reversion of our concepts of personal activity to a primitive model of bodily contact and propulsion. This holds true even of the use here of the notion of a course of action. The relevant facts are that not every action is, or is part of, a course of action and that only *some* 'motivated' actions can be construed as attempts to obtain a desired effect through the completion of a complex, antecedent labor. In contrast, the notion of a course of action is used by Hempel and Oppenheim as if it were the same as that of an action *simpliciter*. One may thus be led to regard *all* motivated action as a finite chain of events, initiated in the hope that the last event in the chain will have a certain anticipated payoff. Since a motivated action (to appropriate one way of putting it) is alleged to be one such that the moving principle is literally in the agent, it follows not only that that which accounts for the action is prior to and distinct from the behavior as such but also that the determining condition must be an inner process. Much the same holds true of the effect achieved, in the same passage, by their setting off "present behavior" against "future event of attaining [a] goal." [21] Again, it gives a false color to the whole argument to illuminate the workings of 'motivation' by projection from this one source of examples.

It is further regrettable that 'course of action' should have been introduced in this way into their argument, in that consideration of a genuine case of carrying through a course of action (say, a rococo swindle) might conveniently provide some sense of difference between 'intention' and 'purpose'. This, I have suggested, is a difference their terms, especially "motivation" and "motivated behavior," serve to obliterate. Given an act which *is* a course of action, one might naturally regard the last stage in this course (gaining possession of the real diamonds) as its purpose, and so as distinguishable from the entire proceeding regarded as the perpetrator's intention.

What we have been concerned with throughout in this inspection of the terms of Hempel and Oppenheim's argument is a set of preconceptions betrayed by those expressions. The rationale for the deployment of those expressions is not stated, but at most suggested. One can only guess, therefore, that a remote but controlling source of such a program is the campaign to discredit the hypothesis of action at a distance. At least this might account for the bent of their anxieties. [22]

21. "The Logic of Explanation," p. 327.
22. I mean such as are manifest in saying, "our formulations above intentionally use the crude terminology frequently applied in philosophical arguments concerning the applicability of causal explanation to purposive behavior, [rather than being] couched in behavioristic terms [which avoid] reference to 'motives' and the like" (*ibid.,* p. 328 n). Elsewhere, Hempel permits himself to speak of "the *vague* general procedure of explanation by reasons" ("Rational Action,"

Finally, I should like to conclude this part with an observation only obliquely concerned with the foregoing discussion. Occasionally in this study I make use of the convenient expression "the agent," to mean simply the person doing the thing in question. This use of the notion of an agent is standard practice in moral philosophy. The reason for the practice, of course, is that at one time the quite general sense of "agent," in its contrast with "patient," was unmistakable. But it is conceivable that now either of two more specific senses may intrude, with unwelcome if unnoticed effect. From an agent as a person driving or leading, hence generally one who acts or does something, came the extension beyond persons to the notion of (a) that which causes a certain effect or produces a certain result, e.g., something which makes something else happen. There is also the derivative application to one who is a deputy, or generally (b) that which is acting at the behest of, or under the strict control of, something else. Both (a) and (b) have figured in philosophical remarks I have had occasion to criticize, so neither is to be taken as essential to any use of "agent" here. I am only suggesting that the contemporary use of "agent" plays some part in the creation of blindness to bad theory. My precaution may be unnecessary. At any rate, it is because of the possible intrusion that I have more often, for example, used "actor," even where that is colloquially a forced application.

Part Three

In the remaining chapters we shall turn to intentions. Here too there is a received view to be considered. The pattern for

Proceedings and Addresses of the American Philosophical Association 1961–1962, XXXV, 23; emphasis added).

that view has already been provided by Hempel and Oppenheim, in coupling belief with desire as the effective antecedent of 'motivated' actions. Though less insistently than for motives, theorists typically do attempt to reshape our conception of intentions. There is an interesting difference from their program concerning motives. For intentions, their emphasis is less upon locale and role, greater upon form. Those concerned to find a distinct and acceptable model for intentions, within prevailing theory, usually present them as molecular. Indeed, this analytic reconstruction of intentions as intrinsically complex is so prominent that it may be regarded as the standard view.

The prominence of that analysis suggests it is at least partially correct. So it is, and in the next chapter I shall indicate just how. The standard view, then, is the principle that an intention, as such, is a compound of two elements, each necessary and together sufficient for the product to be an intention. Writers on the law have succeeded in giving this model clear expression. Here is Salmond's lucid statement: "Intention is the purpose or design with which an act is done. It is the foreknowledge of the act, coupled with the desire of it, such foreknowledge and desire being the cause of the act, inasmuch as they fulfill themselves through the operation of the will. An act is intentional if, and in so far as, it exists in idea before it exists in fact, the idea realising itself in the fact because of the desire by which it is accompanied." [23]

One preliminary remark: that these jointly are sufficient implies that "the act" be understood in a certain, perhaps the normal, way. That is, it is understood to refer to something the person in question himself undertakes to do — or, in the rare case, have done to himself. This is to be assumed so as to rule out

23. *Jurisprudence,* 7th ed. (London, 1924), p. 393. Part of this statement is anticipated on p. 382.

the perfectly real situation of both foreseeing and desiring a certain future event in which, say, one's body is being used as a missile; a use, moreover, for which in the particular event the missile is not to be held accountable. The sense of this restriction is what Salmond intends to convey, of course, by the condition phrase, "inasmuch as they fulfill themselves through the operation of the will." This phrase, however, is not acceptable. But then no one phrase expressing that condition could be both comprehensive and informative. What the words are meant to capture is one's sense that the person in question is a significant element *as actor* in this situation, that he is *doing* the thing which he is said both to foresee and to desire. Given that there is no one attribute or mental act which is of the essence of 'doing something', any expression of the informative kind sought can indicate at best that none of an open list of negativing conditions is realized. Certainly the notion invoked above, of 'undertaking to do the thing', is far from adequate. It has only this advantage over Salmond's more familiar idiom, that it has no history of mistaken use.

We now have the standard view before us. Intention is a mental state having two distinguishable moments or aspects; it is that complex state which can most economically be characterized as desirous foreknowledge. It is taken, on this view, to exist prior to its related action and to be productive, normally, of such an action. There are variations of nomenclature or detail among the exponents of this view; for example, as to whether the one element is called "foreknowledge" or "foresight" — Salmond shifts from the first to the second — and whether this is or is not to be regarded as a definite expectation of the foreseen issue.[24] But there is general agreement on

24. Thus, *ibid.,* p. 394. This latter issue, of course, may become an important one in a contested attribution of intent in an actual case.

the two elements, the one some sort of preview of a realizable state of affairs, the other the operative initiation in one's mind of its eventual (perhaps immediate) production or attainment.[25]

25. Here is Holmes' version: "Intent . . . will be found to resolve itself into two things; foresight that certain consequences will follow from an act, and the wish for those consequences working as a motive which induces the act" (*The Common Law* [Boston, 1881], p. 53). He then proceeds to a reduction of 'foresight of consequences': "It is a picture of a future state of things called up by knowledge of the present state of things, the future being viewed as standing to the present in the relation of effect to cause" (*ibid.*).

——————————— V ———————————

The Standard View
of Intentions

Part One

IN THIS CHAPTER I shall deal schematically with the standard view of an intention as desirous foreknowledge (or, e.g., expectant desire). In the course of showing that that view falls short of the facts, I hope also to show how close one interpretation of it comes to being a perspicuous and accurate representation.

I speak of an interpretation of it, since as it stands it is not one view but the concealment under one formula of four possible specifications. That is, the thought of two pairs of items is actually involved, indiscriminately, in that view. Those items are the idea of a particular future state of affairs, of one's doing something (namely, bringing that state of affairs into being),[1]

---

1. Again, any phrase chosen to express the view (in this instance, "bring a state of affairs into being") should be presumed to be overworked, not only inelegant but necessarily inaccurate.

of one's having a certain belief, and of one's having a certain desire. Just what is the object of the 'conation', and just what is the content of that epistemic state, which adherents to this view wish to specify?

To test the standard view, what is required is that we examine the possible combinations of belief (or knowledge, or assumption), desire, action, and future states of affairs which could yield the standard view. These, then, are the candidate elements:

    (i) one's desire that S be the case;[2]

   (ii) one's desire to bring S into being;

  (iii) one's belief that S will be the case;

  (iv) one's belief that one will bring S into being.

None of the four implicitly permitted conjunctions of these elements — of (i) or (ii), and (iii) or (iv) — is finally tenable, but some are more nearly so than others. The least plausible, surely, is the pairing of (i) and (iii). To say that some person intends that some particular thing shall come to be the case (hereafter, "P intends S") is to say something other than that he desires it and that he believes it will be realized. Consider a man who is joyously sure that the latter day is upon us. He need not take the credit.

It seems fair to say that this pairing is not what would be accepted, by a proponent of the standard view, as a happy specification of what he thought he meant by his doctrine. It remains an open question, for the moment, whether one should judge that (i) and (iii) are *part* of what is meant by saying that P intends S. That is, whether this is to say something in addition to saying P desires and believes that S, or something different. I believe it is something different, indeed neither (i) nor (iii).

   2. Where S is some state of affairs, not necessarily the actor's activity (e.g., being the hangman, rather than running for the office).

Two of the remaining possibilities, the conjunction of (i) or (ii) with (iv), can be considered together since they fall for the same reason, the factitiousness of (iv). The claim that, in saying one intends to do a certain thing, one is expressing a belief as to one's own future action can be construed in (at least) the two gramatically conventional ways. Now, to say "I believe I shall . . ." as nothing more than an expression of belief, or knowledge, as to what in fact is likely to transpire with oneself falls short, recognizably, of fully declaring one's intention. Indeed, unusual circumstances are often needed for one to be understood as treating oneself thus objectively.

Yet, to construe it as an expression of one's belief, or knowledge, of one's *determination* to do the thing — properly, by saying "I believe (know) I will . . ." — is doubly implausible, if put forward as a partial analysis of an expression of intention. To say that one believes or knows, not what in simple futurity one will do, but, in conscious distinction, what one is set upon doing, is very infrequent indeed (except, perhaps, as expression of a nascent intention). The most likely moment for making such a statement probably is one of exceptional and difficult self-disclosure, as in a psychoanalytic session. Further, though one may be drawn to interpreting (iv) in this way so as to effect a clear distinction from (iii), the risk the analysis then runs is that of circularity, of smuggling in reference to one's *intention* in the matter.

So far, the result of scrutinizing the possible specifications of the standard analysis of intention is that only the pairing of (ii) and (iii) remains. It may be attractive in its own right, not merely by default. The remaining interpretation comes to this: to say P intends S is to say he desires to make S the case and believes that S will come to pass (through his own doing). For example, to say of Mme de Montespan that she intended to supplant Mlle de la Vallière as Louis' mistress is to say that she desired to do that required of a successful competitor for the office and believed that she would in fact do so (*D.V.*).

Just now I left open the possibility that (i), that P desires that S, is part of a satisfactory analysis of the attribution to P of a certain intention. The possibility of including either (i) or (ii) in such a scheme is blocked, however. What is in the way is just the fact that one may intend to do something one does not desire to do, contrary to (ii), or to be the case, contrary to (i).

Anything done unwillingly, for instance, is something the actor does *not* desire or want to do. Yet, of course, one nonetheless may unwillingly intend to do the thing. In short, importing into the picture an element of desire (or the like) for the thing intended is a denial of the phenomena.[3] Three observations should help make this evident.

The first is that there is no way of specifying adequately what falls under such a rubric as "desire or the like." Wanting to bring S into being, yearning for it, even being drawn reluctantly by the prospect that S: presumably, all these count. But on what principle is the list being drawn? It is no accident that theorists subscribing to the desirous expectation model of intention sometimes treat a term of special discourse *as if* it covered the lot.[4] Yet this will not do, given the appearance, on

3. Prichard comes close to saying this, in saying that "we occasionally will a change to happen without a desire for it to happen" (*Moral Obligation: Essays and Lectures* [Oxford, 1949], p. 195). Unfortunately, the example he then gives is unpersuasive, and the remark is made in the context of deciding whether, in every act, there is "a desire of the change X which we will" or "a desire of the willing of X" (pp. 194–97).

4. For example, "cathexis" or "cathectic attachment" as used by Parsons and Shils in their essay "Values, Motives, and Systems of Action" in *Toward a General Theory of Action* (ed. Talcott Parsons and

that view, of providing conditions for something to be an intention. What is required, and not provided, is a reasonably definite characterization of this condition of 'desire, or the like', or
a rule for the recognition of instances. It should be noted, also,
that the difficulty with the specification of this condition is not
comparable to those routinely attending novel or marginal applications of such a concept as 'a vehicle'.

It is predictable that in reflecting on this question, whether
a desire for S is a constituent in the intention to do or achieve
S, one will be tempted to say that it *must* be the case that one
desires that which one intends. Now, could this question-beg-
ging conviction be at all defended?[5] Only momentarily, I
think, and only by some such Hobbesian contrivance as the
proposal that what one does unwillingly one desires to do 'on
balance'. But again, to insist on the quite general adequacy of
such a formula, overriding any conceivable seeming counter-

Edward Shils [Cambridge, 1951], pp. 47–243). Note the likeness of
Salmond's notion of desirous foreknowledge and the Parsons-Shils
conjunction "cognition of and cathectic attachment to" (p. 111). Something similar to this is in play earlier when they speak of choice and
expectancy as pervading "the actor's system of relations to the object
world" (pp. 67–68). Still earlier in the book, in the general statement
by all nine contributors to the volume, there is a virtual definition of
"cathexis": "Cathexis, the attachment to objects which are gratifying
and rejection of those which are noxious, lies at the root of the selective
nature of action" (p. 5). Nothing would be gained by substituting this
picture of 'attachment' for the notion of desire in the standard view of
intention.

5. Note that it is only the unqualified conviction, that a desire for the
thing intended is intrinsic to every intention, which is in question here.
There is certainly warrant for an occasional and discriminating claim;
for example, that though someone was of two minds about doing that
which he intended yet to do, he nonetheless desired on balance to do it.
We may speak of a balance when we may speak of an opposition, and
so of a weighing.

instances, betrays an a priori preconception. To say that *any-thing* done intentionally is as such something the actor desired on balance (or, 'in some sense', 'to some degree', 'in the last analysis') is a mere restatement of a thesis, not an appeal to the facts. To take an example, it is then a thesis being unfittingly *imposed* on such a common (and simple) sort of explanation as this: Aubrey plunged into the icy waters to save Audrey, whom he saw drowning. The thesis is belied in such a case, provided Aubrey knew the water was icy, loathed being in icy water, and yet responded to the situation without first pondering the net effect for himself of doing so.

Finally, it is not obvious, in some cases, how to give a fitting account of actions undertaken in situations of practical conflict, and this may help account for reluctance to omit (i) or (ii) from an analysis of intention. Consider such circumstances as those sketched by Aristotle in his description of 'mixed' actions.[6] It may seem, for example, that the mariner in jeopardy who jettisons valuable cargo is someone who is both unwilling to do what he did and yet desires to do it. But that would be a misrepresentation of the case. There is room, within Aristotle's useful story, to sort out (a) the mariner's intentional action from both (b) that which he is unwilling to do or suffer and (c) what he does desire. For he (a) jettisoned the cargo even though unhappy at (b) losing (the value of) the goods, in order (c) to save the foundering ship and its passengers. Not surprisingly, what he desires is coincident with his purpose, which was the saving of passengers and ship, seen as achievable. In short, mixed actions do not constitute a class in which the actor desires that which he intends to do, and desires it *in* intending it.[7]

6. *Nicomachean Ethics,* III.i.
7. This is not to say that there are not problems concerning mixed

Part Two

There is a last device, yet to be scouted, for saving at least part of the standard analysis of intention. That is, to weaken the epistemic component, on the ground that "belief" and its congeners are too definite and too suggestive of conscious attention to one's routine future activities. What would fit in well in (iii) or (iv), it might plausibly be suggested, is "assumption."

That this should be thought admissible, let alone required, depends upon the simple view that an assumption is, after all, an unspoken belief. So, to assume that something is the case is to believe that it is so but not to have made an explicit judgment about it. Our immediate task is to test this view. Then we shall apply the result of this examination to intention.

One thing we can agree on is that when P assumes Z (in some practical context), it is not the case that P believes that it is not the case that Z; that is, it is false that P believes that not-Z. Here is where agreement is likely to end. Some philosophical writing conveys a picture of our waking lives — that of sensate, intelligent, and active creatures — as an uninterrupted flow of making and testing assumptions. This sugges-

---

actions, and concerning our understanding of what is said at this point in the *Nicomachean Ethics* about them. For one thing, there is the import of the general formula for mixed actions, "things that are done from fear of greater evils or for some noble object" (Ross trans.). The subsequent question, whether such actions are voluntary or involuntary, can only arise, as it does, in a context which concedes the possibility that such actions are done under a compulsion sufficiently like an overpowering wind. Yet in what follows we are given nothing comparable to the fear which 'moves' the man threatened by tyrant or storm, to account *in a similar way* for an action done for a noble purpose. Ordinary good deeds, even those involving real sacrifice, will not do, as instances.

tion is supportable, I think, only on the premise that its being false that P believes that not-Z is equivalent to P's believing that Z. Yet this is not so, plainly. One who has no thoughts whatsoever as to which is the highest mountain in the Western Hemisphere is certainly one of whom it would be false to say for that reason that he believes Aconcagua is the highest.

What, then, is essential to P's assuming Z? Consider a man bitten by a camel. Let us say this man (call him Francis) believes he has an infallibly winning way with birds and beasts; that at some time in the past he has been told, and credibly, that this kind of animal was prone to biting people; that Francis could have recalled this information, if prompted, though it was not in his mind when he reached up to pat the camel; and, finally, that it was not the case that, prior to being bitten, Francis believed he would be bitten. If these conditions obtain, then it is true that Francis assumed he would not be bitten. If, however, Francis was quite ignorant of the likelihood of being bitten by a camel, or otherwise rejected by the world of brutes, it would not follow that he had assumed he would not be bitten, though it would still be the case that it was false he had believed he would be bitten.

Two points emerging from the variants of this episode deserve to be noted straight off. One, surely indisputable on any analysis of assuming, is that the truth or falsity of "Z" (e.g., "I shall not be bitten") is immaterial to its being, or failing to be, the case that P assumed Z. Note that, under the conditions first listed, it would be true that Francis assumed he would not be bitten, whether in the event he was or was not bitten. The other observation is that one part of the first story is actually superfluous. It is not a condition, bearing on Francis' assuming the camel would not bite, whether or not the warning about camels was in his mind at the moment of acting.

Our result, then, can be formulated in the following way: to say that P assumes Z is to say

    (a) It is not the case that P believes that not-Z;

yet

    (b) P believes there is some (genuine but insufficient) reason for him to believe that not-Z.

The only important general principle which depends on this is that it shows that no great part of one's actions, let alone one and all, is the product of assumption. (Apart from our limited interest here in this observation, it is worth recording because of the number and confidence of those who have denied it.) Though I may act in no doubt of their reliability, I do not thereby show I *assumed* the floorboards, or your assurances, are reliable. For that, I need some specific reason to give them little weight. The genuineness of a reason for believing that not-Z is not certified by the logical possibility that not-Z. Hence, in Francis' case, the complexity of the facts jointly satisfying (b): he believes what he was told about camel misanthropy but it is not the case that he believes that his peculiar gift is at all likely to fail him in this instance. Note, however, that it is not the case that he believes there is *no* real chance of failure on this occasion.[8] One may be perfectly confident in one's assumption, yet, should it be called into question, consistently admit the possibility of being wrong. Just as one does not assume to be the case that which one doubts, so neither does one assume that which one has no reason to doubt.

An additional benefit of this analysis is that it enables us to give a quite definite location, as it were, to the ancillary notion

---

8. To say "it is not the case that he believes . . ." is maladroit; by it I mean just "he does not believe. . . ." But in most contexts "he does not believe . . ." is rightly taken as the positive attribution to the subject of a contrary belief.

of the reasonableness of an assumption. If it were the case that to have assumed that Z is to believe (*sotto voce*) that Z, then the notion of the reasonableness of an assumption would be made to seem rather loose, which it is not. It might be thought, along that line, that the reasonableness of my assumption, that Z, depended on what *sort* of state of affairs Z is taken to be (namely, unproblematic), or even, at least to some degree, on Z's being the case. We are now in a position, on the contrary, to see why $R(P$ assumes $Z)$ — i.e., the reasonableness of P's assumption that Z — is a function neither of Z's being unremarkable nor of Z's being the case. Obviously, it turns upon the reasonableness of P's not believing that not-Z; but also, and perhaps less obviously, upon the reasonableness of P's believing there are (insufficient) grounds to believe that not-Z.

With its parts now on display, the notion of assumption does not present itself attractively as an ingredient in that of intention. To demonstrate that this is so, however, does require actually fitting in the notion of assumption and then examining the result. Here we come upon complication, since there are a number of ways, perhaps equally plausible, to accommodate mention of an assumption within a revised standard version of intention. I shall lay out for consideration two likely proposals.

The simpler one is that when P intends S,

(c) P desires to do S;

(d) P assumes that he will do S.

A more elaborate fabrication is that when P intends S,

(e) P desires that S;

(f) P assumes that if M, then S;[9]

(g) P believes he will do M.

9. Where M is some way of doing S, or means of bringing it about that S.

Both (c) and (e) are dubious entries, for the reasons given before concerning any *ad hoc* insistence that one must desire that which one intends. The second element, (d), is to be rejected on a different ground: when P intends S it is not necessarily the case that P believes there is some (gratifyingly feeble) reason to believe he will in fact not do S. Similarly for (f): when P intends S it is not necessarily the case that he believes there is some reason to believe that it is not the case that if M, then S. In addition, (f) is made unacceptable by the fact that not every intentional action is an end for the realization of which the actor makes use of some means. If, as a defiant recruit, I deliberately turn my head, having been told not to by the drill instructor, I have not chosen a means to the perverse end of turning my head (though I may have a purpose, of course, in turning my head).

By now, we should expect no rescue, for the standard view of intention, from notions close to that of assumption. 'Expectation', for instance, is no more redemptive of that view than is 'assumption'. There is at least one parallel, disabling, feature: when P intends S, he does not necessarily expect S to be the case, even though neither does he expect it not to be the case. Yet there is one further possibility concerning the analysis of an intention which deserves a trial in this context. It can be expressed as a principle concerning what part or stage it is in an action which can strictly be attributed to the actor.[10] Prich-

10. As it was in the ambiguous remark by Richard Price we noted above (p. 27). There is a strong instance in this Stoic affirmation by Montaigne, in one of the early essays ("That Intention is Judge of our Actions"): "We cannot be bound beyond our powers and means. For this reason — that we have no power to effect and accomplish, that there is nothing really in our power but will [les effects et executions ne sont aucunement en nostre puissance et . . . il n'y a rien . . . en nostre puissance que la volonté] — all man's rules of duty are neces-

ard submits to this restriction when he tells us that an action is "an activity of willing some change."[11] Here we shall test it in the form of the conviction that when a man expresses an intention he does indeed claim a certain piece of knowledge. Specifically, it is supposed, he purports to know (at any rate, believe) at least what he will *try* to do at a certain juncture.

What, then, is involved in saying of an individual that he tried to do a certain thing? The following is an approximate synopsis: that he at least began to do the thing in question (e.g., by turning the doorknob) and that he believed there was reason to expect he might not succeed in doing it. The first condition is familiar, certainly, given the need both in practice and in legal theory to distinguish preparation from attempt.[12] It is

---

sarily founded and established in our will" (*The Complete Works of Montaigne,* trans. D. M. Frame [Stanford, 1957], p. 20). This is set within a discussion which is more to his credit, because less doctrinaire. He brackets his extreme principle "qu'il n'y a rien [vraiment] en nostre puissance que la volonté" by remarks (concerning two famous and contrasting episodes of trust betrayed) which are interpretable in a quite different and reasonable way.

Consider this argument: (1) the only sort of thing it is logically possible for one to do is that which is truly within one's power to do; (2) but only one's *will* is truly within one's power; (3) therefore, strictly speaking, the only sort of thing one *does* is to perform acts of will.

Where is this position (call it The Argument for Least Action) fully articulated? The second premise (Montaigne) and the conclusion (Richard Price, James) are well represented, but I am ignorant of any appearance of the ensemble.

11. *Moral Obligation,* p. 193. Not surprisingly, Prichard goes on, with specific use of the illustration of 'willing' a table across the room to move toward oneself, to endorse James' inflation of the notion of willing something to happen.

12. It is because this condition obtains that Prichard is right in saying that "what we call trying to do something is as much doing something as what we ordinarily call doing something, although the word 'trying' suggests that it is not." The unsound reason Prichard gives is

the second condition that bears on our present concern. Just what is its bearing can be shown by noting three evident truths about the concept of trying which this analysis preserves.

The first is that one may either succeed or fail when one tries. This is worth remarking only because there is some occasional temptation to suggest that saying someone tried to do a certain thing is tantamount to saying he failed. (It has been said, for instance, that attempt implies failure.)[13] James gives this recipe, by now well known, to produce "a certain illusion": "Close the patient's eyes, hold his anaesthetic arm still, and tell him to raise his hand to his head; and when he opens his eyes he will be astonished to find that the movement has not taken place."[14] A commentator has said that

One might well say that he had at least *tried* to move it. And hence that what is left over is . . . "I tried to move my arm." But this is unsatisfactory in that the patient may be unaware of any difficulty in moving his hand. . . . From the patient's point of view it is not as if he had to try to move his hand, but as if he could actually, and easily, move it — or, at least, it is like this to him until he opens his eyes. In short, "He tried to

---

rather that trying "is the willing a change" (*Moral Obligation,* p. 196).

13. Jerome Hall, *General Principles of Criminal Law,* 2d ed. (Indianapolis, 1960), p. 577. This is not redeemed by his going on (in a note) to say, in effect, that it is only when criminal attempts *are* unsuccessful that the law is concerned with them as such. This authority may well be warranted, however, in alluding to "the usual assumption that attempts fail." Consider this dictum of an American state supreme court, a definition expressly not limited to those attempts which are of legal concern: "An attempt, in general, is an overt act done in pursuance of an intent to do a specific thing, tending to the end but falling short of complete accomplishment of it" (*Commonwealth* v. *Egan,* 190 Pa. 21 [1899]).

14. *The Principles of Psychology,* 2 vols. (New York, 1890), II, 105.

move his hand" describes not so much what the patient did as what he did not do: he failed to qualify for the description "He moved his hand." [15]

This is so nearly right it is worth clearing up. It is just not the case that "he tried to move his hand" *describes* what someone did not do, however plainly, in appropriate narrative circumstances, it *conveys* his failure. Vesey is insufficiently obstinate; he should have stuck by his insight that, *since* the patient knows of no impediment to his moving his hand, "it is not as if he had to try to move his hand." Vesey's problem, of course, is that he thinks there is reason both to say and to deny that the patient tried to move his hand; or that there is reason to balk at "I tried . . ." while accepting "He tried. . . ." But this dilemma is unreal, and Vesey himself has shown why. It is *false* that one might *well* say that the patient had at least tried to move his hand.

What might one well say? That he thought he had moved it. At least, with regard to such an extraordinary episode, one cannot go further in answering the question "What did he do?" James does in effect describe such a person as believing he had done the thing requested ("[such persons] are apt to feel as if the movement had actually taken place"). But James also tries, as it were, to answer the question "But what did he *do?*" by describing the case as one in which "we will to execute a movement." [16]

The second is that the way in which one goes about (beginning to do) the thing is not intrinsic to its being a case of trying to do it. The style of one's attempt may vary from great hesitation to perfectly smooth performance, and so contributes

15. G. N. A. Vesey, "Volition," *Philosophy*, XXXVI (1961), 353.
16. *The Principles of Psychology*, II, 105.

nothing in itself to the act's being one of trying. The third is that not everything one does, even when it is successful, foreseen, and agreeable, is something one believes there is some particular reason to believe one may fail to bring off. This surely counts decisively against the supposition that when P intends S, he thereby knows (at least) what he will try to do. On some occasions, of course, but only some, P's intention is that of *trying* to do or achieve S; but that has no special significance for the present question.

There is one important respect in which the analysis proposed is open to attack. This is that it is arguable that to say P will try to T cannot entail P knows (even, believes) this. Perhaps you may correctly say of me that I am about to try to light the candle, even when you know that a certain real, present possibility of failure has never occurred to me. It may be enough that you believe I am running such a risk. Accordingly, it might be well argued that the second condition set out above should hold, not that the actor (necessarily) believes there is reason to anticipate failure, but rather simply that there *is* such reason, whether or not he appreciates it. Still, whichever version of this condition holds will have as a consequence that trying, and so the knowledge of it, is only a sometime thing, not an aspect of every routine act.

The result of our critique of the standard view of intention, taking it in various favoring and definite ways, is negative. There is no tenable interpretation of it, within the limits of the core notion of desirous foreknowledge. It is not entirely a Potemkin village, however. As conceded earlier, there is some substance behind that notion. Take one of the more nearly passable combinations of its candidate elements, the alliance of (ii) and (iii); that is, again, the proposal that to say P intends S is to say P desires to make S the case and believes that S will come to pass, through his own doing. The appeal of this proposal is not entirely dispelled by recognizing its faults. Two reasons, I imagine, can be offered in explanation of this. One is to its credit, the other is not.

The first is that the standard version is certainly not unrelated to the facts. To the contrary, it is the reverse aspect of a certain complex fact: when P intends S, it is neither the case that P *ipso facto* desires *not* to bring S into being nor that P believes S will not come to pass. The second reason, I suggest, is connected with the first. It is the preconception that when speaking of P's intention we *must* have in view the obverse, a positive desire on his part to do or achieve S, joined with a belief that in fact he will gratify this desire, conditions permitting. Again, in the background would seem to be the primitive conviction that citation of an intention could not account for an act if the intention were not a quasi-propulsive inner episode, or essentially related to one.

Accordingly, it will be the business of the remaining two chapters to show that such convictions are wrong. The method of demonstration will be familiar, that of showing the thing must be possible, since it is actual. What follows will be similar, in plan and materials, to the exhibition in Chapter I of actual motive-explanations. There, the end was principally that of coming to see, unblinded by conventions, what sorts of things are in fact cited as motives for actions. So here we will examine a brief schedule of accounts adverting to an actor's intention, accounts likewise found in neutral waters, mostly those of historical narrative. Here too the specimens taken up for comment will be chosen for their probative value. They are useful in breaking the hold of another theory-born restriction upon our capacity to appreciate matters already before us.

There is no rule, of course, for the production of all possible objections to the picture of intentions as (certain) actions. Still, on review, a high proportion (perhaps all) of such objections are seen to be of one of two general sorts: that a man's intentions are as such *categorically* distinguishable from his actions, or that his as yet unfulfilled intentions are *temporally* distinguishable from the relevant deeds. Either one can appear as the complaint that an intention must be a ('positive') inner state of *some* sort, or that an as yet unfulfilled intention *cannot* be an action in the offing. Considerations seeming to sustain the latter will weaken one's resistance to the former.

This sorting into two general kinds is at least a useful way of ordering the theorist's misgivings. It may well be that there is fundamentally only one ground of objection, the brute belief that intentions and (outer) acts are different in kind. For instance, saying that intentions, like parents, have lived a life of their own prior to our actions could be simply a way of pretending to show the necessity of a difference in kind. If so, the proposed separation of objections can be regarded as no more than a temporary divorce of convenience.

The selection of bits of historical narrative to be considered is governed by the aim of showing (not less than) that typical accounts *need* not be accommodated to the inner-state theory. What forces itself upon our notice, when such samples are looked at steadily, is that there is nothing in those accounts which obliges us to regard intentions as inner states or processes.

VI

The Publicity
of Intentions

Part One

A USEFUL WAY TO BEGIN is to note what is plain but neglected. In describing and explaining human activities, we often do more, when a person's intentions are brought into the picture, than merely attribute a particular intention to him, or deny its attributability. Among the multitude of (call them) intention-invocations we find in historical narrative, certain distinct types naturally sort themselves out. Any inventory of such types would include (1) the claim that *some* (perhaps quite unspecified) thing must have been intended by what was done; and (2) the claim that there is a genuine possibility that a particular sort of thing, here named or described by the historian, *may* have been intended; and (3) the claim that a spcified thing, and so not a certain other, *was* (or, *must* have been) the intention in view.

These types form a sequence, ordered with respect to a

specification of the identity of the intention and the conclusive-
ness of the argument as to the existence of an intention. The
first and third types are more illuminating, for our present
purposes. Here is an example of (1):

> The new Secretariat consisted of Stalin, Kaganovich, Kirov, and
> Zhdanov. . . . There was one notable fact about the laconic an-
> nouncement of this election which appeared in the press. Stalin,
> who since 1922 had invariably been described as "General Secre-
> tary," was now described only as "Secretary." Such points of formal
> title are always a matter of scrupulous care in Soviet practice. Any
> question of error in Stalin's title is quite inconceivable . . .[1]

In this instance of that type, as it happens, the historian goes
on to tell us, in the latter half of the last sentence quoted, just
what the intention was: "it was plain to all that some diminution of authority was thereby intended." In effect, this addition
transforms the account from one of our first type to one of
something close to the third type. What is more important to
note is that the author cannot be represented as saying that the
change of title stands to the diminution of authority merely
as means to end. The preceding statements, especially the observation of the Byzantine care exercised in such matters, make
plain that the title change in some measure *constituted,* as well
perhaps as effected and reflected, a diminution of Stalin's authority. The thing done *is* the intention.

We can arrive at the same point by a different route. That
is to ask what inference, if any, is to be ascribed to the historian in arriving at the attribution of a certain intention to
those responsible for the change of title. Certainly this account
rests upon an inference concerning their intention. It is a firm

1. Leonard Shapiro, *The Communist Party of the Soviet Union* (New
York, 1960), p. 398.

inference, from the known relevant practices, to the *character* of the thing done. It is not a blind passage, from the thing done to the 'inner' antecedents of the public act. Nor can such a misrepresentation of the workings of this explanation be introduced, say, under cover of noting the difference between the changing of Stalin's title (or, the ordering of that change), and the changed title. For that difference can be accommodated to the particular claims in Shapiro's account only by treating the ordering of the change as the way to the achievement of the intention itself, namely, the diminution of authority constituted by the restriction in title.

The following would be an example of (2). A historian writing on medieval English society wishes to illustrate the bitterness aroused by the forest law. She notes that in a mid-thirteenth-century account of a contemporary episode of deer poaching in Northampton, mention is made of the poachers' having impaled the head of a buck on a stake in a clearing, jaws agape, facing south.[2] The historian then suggests it is significant that the area had once been the Danes' land, given a similar and consciously contemptuous practice on their part.[3] On these facts, and perhaps others about the survival of certain beliefs and rituals in submerged cultures, the historian could rightly say we are warranted in supposing the poachers may well have intended their bizarre act as a gesture of defiance to the king in the south.

The same narrative, suitably abbreviated, will supply a missing member of this series of types of intention-invocation, one as yet unmentioned. Since this addition will close the series, it

2. I adapt this story from D. L. Stenton, *English Society in the Early Middle Ages* (*1066–1307*) (Harmondsworth, 1952), p. 111.

3. "Those in the saga world who wished to show contempt for others set a horse's head on a hazel pole and made it gape towards them" (*ibid.*, p. 281, n.196).

will serve also to help make fully explicit the way in which the series is constructed. Suppose, then, that the historian had only reported the act of impaling the deer head, and confessed having no idea of any specific intention in the light of which we could understand the act. It would still have been intelligible of her to remark that the poachers may have had some intention in so doing, it being unlikely that that was something they did for no reason, out of no conception whatsoever of meaning in the act. This kind of observation, that it is reasonable to suppose the thing done may have been connected with *some* intention, would stand at the beginning of our previous list, as an intention-invocation of type (o).

We can now lay out fully the principle of the progression. In types (o)–(3), there appear two kinds of assertion about the *existence* of an intention, namely, either (a) that there may be (or may have been) one involved, or (b) that there definitely was, or must have been, such. Similarly, there appear also two kinds of assertion as to *what* the intention was, namely, either (c) that what the intention was is a blank, unspecifiable by the reporter, or (d) that the intention was, or must have been, of such-and-such a (more or less nearly individuating) kind. Accordingly, type (o) is in effect the conjunction of (a) and (c); type (1), of (b) and (c);[4] type (2), of (a) and (d);[5] and type (3), of (b) and (d). It is apparent also that this series is a consistent ordering.[6]

4. That is, supposing Shapiro had stopped short of saying what the change in Stalin's title constituted.

5. In the example, again, the claim that the impaling of the head may have been a gesture of defiance to the king and his oppressive law.

6. As for the end points, what is now first in the list, (o), contains no unqualified assertion as to the existence or nature of an intention in the case, whereas (3) is categorical with respect both to the existence

Motive and Intention

Here is an elaborate, but essentially simple, instance of (3):

A picture by . . . Maffei, representing a handsome young woman with a sword in her right hand, and in her left a charger on which rests the head of a beheaded man, has been published as a portrayal of Salome with the head of John the Baptist. In fact the Bible states that the head of John the Baptist was brought to Salome on a charger. But what about the sword? Salome did not decapitate John the Baptist with her own hands. Now the Bible tells us about another handsome woman in connection with the decapitation of a man, namely Judith. In this case the situation is exactly reversed. The sword would be correct because Judith beheaded Holofernes with her own hand, but the charger would not agree with the Judith theme because the text explicitly states that the head of Holofernes was put into a sack. Thus we have two literary sources applicable to our picture with equal right and equal consistency. . . . Fortunately . . . we [can] correct and control our knowledge of literary sources by inquiring into the . . . history of types. In the case at hand we shall have to ask whether there were, before Francesco Maffei painted his picture, any unquestionable portrayals of Judith (unquestionable because they would include, for instance, Judith's maid) with unjustified chargers; or any unquestionable portrayals of Salome (unquestionable because they would include, for instance, Salome's parents) with unjustified swords. And lo! while we cannot adduce a single Salome with a sword, we encounter . . . several sixteenth-century paintings depicting Judith with a charger; there was a *type* of 'Judith with a charger', but there was no type of 'Salome with a sword'. From this we can safely conclude that Maffei's picture, too, represents Judith, and not, as has been assumed, Salome.[7]

---

and nature of the intention. As for the middle pair, the ordering also seems reasonable, in that there is at least qualified assertion made in (2) both as to the existence and as to the nature of the intention, whereas (1) is noncommittal as to the nature of the intention ascribed.

7. Erwin Panofsky, *Studies in Iconology: Humanistic Themes in the Art of the Renaissance* (New York, 1939), pp. 12–13, reprinted by permission of Harper and Row. It should be noted, in order to convey

We may take Panofsky's splendidly explicit argument as one about Maffei's intention, a reasoned claim of type (3). For us, the salient point is that the argument is about the (subject of the) *painting*. It is not, even by indirection, concerned with some defunct process in the artist's mind. Though there may be considerations which could weaken our confidence in Panofsky's verdict, they would be facts of a similar public order, similarly bearing on one's appreciation of the visible object.

Now, one can indeed imagine the internalist resorting to a customary sort of response at this point. In particular, that of citing the logical possibility of Maffei's having declared, just as he finished, that he had portrayed Salome. But this does not begin to be a telling claim, in and of itself. For one thing, if Panofsky has his facts straight about the earlier associations of the relevant motifs, and if his implicit assurance about the conventionality of such matters is reliable, it is in fact extremely unlikely that Maffei thought or said such a thing. What is more important to realize is that it just is not the case that what (let us suppose) he said would settle the matter, upsetting Panofsky's conclusion. The more likely way we should adjust such an incongruous avowal to all the items Panofsky relies upon would be to take it as a *mistake* on Maffei's part, even, should he have repeated it, a deeply interesting self-betrayal.

This is not to say that Maffei's word could not possibly carry weight, even enough to upset the verdict. It is only to note

the full strength of Panofsky's argument, that he then goes on to show why "the motif of a charger could more easily be substituted for the motif of a sack in an image of Judith, than the motif of a sword could have penetrated into an image of Salome" (p. 14). The argument as a whole is given in substantiation of Panofsky's general admonition that it is "impossible for us to give a correct *iconographical analysis* by indiscriminately applying our literary knowledge to the motifs. . . ."

that such an avowal would not be self-authenticating. It would not even be especially privileged testimony, taken by itself, as to the true character of a specimen of the exceptionally conservative practice which this picture represents. Such a declaration. could be taken seriously only if coherent with additional facts of the varied and public sort Panofsky adduces, or indicative of a new perspective on those already arrayed by the historian. And that is why the fact that the chance of there having been such an announcement, sincerely made, is very small really does counter a protest based on the undeniable *possibility* of Maffei's having made the announcement. For the very conditions which make improbable such an occurrence make it unreasonable in these circumstances to treat the sincerity of the speaker as a reliable sign of the truth of what he said.

Part Two

We have noted before that the internal-agitation theory of motives obliges one who holds it to *construe* a good proportion of motive-explanations; that is, not to take such an exoteric form of account at face value. Rather, the scrupulous adherent to the theory would be forced to make an a priori claim about our success in concocting and understanding motive-explanations. That claim is that usually one drastically but silently revises such accounts to conform to the one kind held canonical by the theory. So also with the inner-state theory of intentions. Quite apart from particular infidelities to the facts, there is a standing impediment to its use. Its adoption implies that, contrary to appearances, one *interprets* the greater number of intention-invocations; specifically, that one severely allegorizes what in fact is said. One is supposed to do so by regarding the reported fact — the diminution or ritual defiance of authority, the portrayal of a certain figure — as only a sign of covert processes.

It will go a long way to demythologizing the relation of intention and act to recognize the genuineness of a simple distinction. Call it the difference of a deed from its character. By "the character of the deed" I mean what the deed may be taken as *being*, by a relevantly knowledgeable person. Accordingly, by "the deed" I mean only the thing done taken under some description not partial to a particular reading of its character. Now, for simple cases it raises no problems to say that the character assigned to the deed *is* the intention. Odysseus' intention in twisting the heated olive pole *was* the damaging of Polyphemos' eye. One difficulty raised in problematic cases is that of demonstrating, as in Panofsky's argument, the assignability of a certain character to the thing done.

One immediate use to which we may put this distinction is to help clarify what it is we are told when we are told, as commonly, that someone knew what he was doing. This claim is typically made, of course, when some question has been raised, or anticipated, about the actor's care or competence in his particular role. Here, in a summary account of the doctoring of the Ems Telegram, is a standard example of such a claim: "The King of Prussia seems to have behaved with complete propriety, but of course refused Benedetti's demand for a declaration which would have been almost an admission of his own dishonesty. Bismarck, to whom the episode was reported, saw his opportunity and gave the press a short statement which read like a brusque rebuff from William I to Benedetti: there is no doubt that he knew what he was doing." [8] The more sig-

8. Alfred Cobban, *A History of Modern France,* 3d ed., 3 vols. (Baltimore, 1963-65), II, 201.

nificant part of this judgment is not that Bismarck knew what he was doing but rather that there is no doubt about it. For the implied admission is that one may *not* know what one is doing, even in situations where one is working with an open eye. Thus our sense of just what "what he was doing" refers to — of what it is the actor is said to know, when, as here, he is simply said to know what he is doing — is very much governed by what question about the actor the context raises.

Here there is no problem raised as to whether or not Bismarck knew he was giving the press a statement, although that precisely could have been the question brought to life by a different narrative environment. Rather, the form of possible ignorance of which Bismarck is here acquitted is indicated at first generally by speaking of circumstances which he would regard as providing an opportunity, and then specifically by saying how the statement would be taken by the touchy French. "What he was doing," then, is associated by the particular structure of this account with the act of making it seem the king was deliberately creating a provocation, forcing the diplomatic crisis to a more extreme stage.

I have claimed that this one example is representative. If it is so, then what it is one claims to know (or is credited with knowing), in knowing what one is doing, is nothing other than the character of one's deed.[9] A comparison may now reinforce one's sense of the *complexity* of understanding which can be accommodated under the notion of knowing, or seeing, what one is doing. Consider what (in the determination of the historian) it is that Commons perceived, at a certain juncture:

9. And *not,* as such, the likely *consequences* of what one is doing, however closely in a particular instance knowledge of the one may undeniably be bound to knowledge of the other.

The King's frank hostility had its effect. In the House of Commons . . . they resolved not to wait any more for his consent to the Militia Bill, but to issue it themselves as an Ordinance, and to take over the defence of the Kingdom without more ado. They perceived the significance of what they were doing, for this was to proclaim the power of Parliament to act for the good of the country independently of the King. . . . By this action Parliament assumed to itself sovereign authority, thus indicating that the King's power, as King, was not the same as his personal and natural power.[10]

Here, "the significance of what they were doing" is strictly comparable to "what he was doing" in the Ems Telegram example. For here (2′), to proclaim the power of Parliament to act for the good of the country independently of the king, is to (1′), to issue a Militia Bill as an ordinance, as (2), to make it seem the king of Prussia had brusquely rebuffed the ambassador of France, is to (1), to give the press a certain statement in the king's name.

It is worth emphasizing at this point what might otherwise go unnoticed. In an essential respect, the notion of 'knowing what one is doing' is like that of 'taking action'. Just as 'taking action' is understood as doing a (more or less) restricted *kind* of thing, so 'knowing what one is doing' is the acceptance, from the *limited* number of reasonable versions, of a particular appreciation of one's actions. In each case the subject, so undetermined by the naming expressions themselves, is compensatingly delimited by their surrounding discourse.

One of the commitments implicit in the way the distinction of character from deed was drawn has now been brought into the open. That is, that there is nothing in that distinction confining a deed to a simple character, or to only one proper char-

10. C. V. Wedgwood, *The King's War, 1641–1647* (New York, 1959), pp. 72–73.

acter. The facts, plainly, would not allow of it. Often we have a grave opportunity (or comic chance) of recognizing several characters as reasonably assignable to a given deed. One need consider only The Act. Milton provides a virtuoso description of what Adam and Woman *did,* in their joint deed of tasting the fruit forbidden them.[11] Indeed, this feature of the way the distinction is drawn, the appeal to the judgment of a relevantly knowledgeable person, helps account for a good deal, including the very possibility of discrepant declarations as to what a person's intention is or was, as well as the possibility of someone's sincerely claiming to be ignorant of his own intention.

The heart of the matter is that different persons are enabled to put divergent yet reasonable constructions upon a deed by giving differential consideration to pertinent circumstances. Many instances in which a historian finds it useful to declare how the actor took his own deed will illustrate this. Here is a

---

11. I take Milton's notion of that which is 'included in', or 'comprehended by', the act as that of what I have called "the character" of the deed. This is what he says:

"What sin . . . was not included in this one act? It comprehended at once distrust in the divine veracity, and a proportionate credulity in the assurances of Satan; unbelief; ingratitude; disobedience; gluttony; in the man excessive uxoriousness, in the woman a want of proper regard for her husband, in both an insensibility to the welfare of their offspring . . . ; parricide, theft, invasion of the rights of others, sacrilege, deceit, presumption to aspiring to divine attributes, fraud in the means employed to attain the object, pride, and arrogance" (*A Treatise on Christian Doctrine,* Bk. I, Chap. 11 [*The Prose Works of John Milton,* Vol. IV, trans. C. R. Sumner (London, 1891), p. 254]).

True, we cannot accept quite all these items, such as the parricide listed, as descriptions of the one act. But it is more important to emphasize that, with such exceptions, the relation of 'inclusion' or 'comprehension' which Milton invokes is decidedly not that of an act to its sequelae.

simple example, only seemingly complicated by the irrelevant bulk of the 'deed' on display: "By his policy . . . Pym had brought the Crown under the control of Parliament. . . . He did not advertise his achievement as a revolution and it did not appear so to him. He believed that he was restoring the ancient balance between the sovereign and the people glorified under Elizabeth." [12] When the historian states what it is that someone held himself to have done, we often need help to see the deed as the actor does. His own expression of belief may be inadequate testimony, taken by itself. In this particular case, moreover, the historian disagrees with the actor's appreciation of his achievement. Thus the problem of making credible her report that Pym assigned such-and-such a character to his own deed is especially urgent; it is necessary for her as for us to discover the *ground* of Pym's belief, and to find it intelligible that such a belief could have been sustained on that ground. This is why it is critical for her to suggest (as she does), and for us to find sufficiently reasonable, that Pym had been deeply impressed by Coke's recently published work on (what Coke claimed to be) the meaning of Magna Carta.

There is a kind of remark about intention and action which demands particular care in analysis. We are now in a convenient position to examine it. I mean the assertion that someone had no intention of doing a certain sort of thing but nonetheless had (freely) done it, or was firmly on the way to having done it. Obviously, this kind of report presents no problem for an inner-state theory of intentions, especially not to one brazenly embracing the thesis that the connection of intention to act, at least from our empirical disadvantage-point, is a contingent one. Here, in an account of the developing imperatives

12. C. V. Wedgwood, *The King's Peace, 1637–1641* (New York, 1956), p. 433.

of government faced by Alexander, is an example of the weaker version of this problematic sort of account: "There is nothing to show that he had any intention of doing away with Greek freedom; Craterus' instructions to supervise the freedom of the Hellenes . . . show that the exiles decree was treated as an exceptional measure and that the League was to continue as before. But Alexander had taken the first step on the road of interference in the internal affairs of the cities; and he had sworn not to interfere." [13] What is crucial to show is just how, and how well, the second half of the first quoted sentence functions. In this account, the deed to be appraised is Alexander's having ordered the cities of the League of Corinth, in 324, to take back their respective political exiles. It is this deed which makes the intention in question a live issue. Thus, by saying that there is nothing to show Alexander did have that intention, Tarn is in effect committed to making it possible for us to believe Alexander saw that deed as having a character other than that of interference. It is just this which the second part of the first sentence contrives, the reconciliation of the fact of the exiles decree with the alleged continued adherence by Alexander to the general principle of noninterference.

As it happens, how successful we judge the reference to the instructions to Craterus to be is affected by our resolution of a possible ambiguity in the first sentence as a whole. That is, it is a question whether we take Tarn's claim that there is nothing to show Alexander had the intention *strictly,* as saying just that there is no evidence to that effect; or whether we take it as a positive existential claim, namely, that Alexander had a different intention, one incompatible with the intention of

13. W. W. Tarn, *Alexander the Great,* 2 vols. (Cambridge, 1948), I, 113–14. Craterus was sent back to replace Antipater in overseeing the affairs of Greece for Alexander.

interfering. I take it the latter half of the sentence obliges us to construe the first part in this second way. Yet the passage does not state what Tarn thought Alexander's intention to be. Even so, it is plainly implicit here that the intention was the limited one of minimizing internal dissension among the non-Asiatic Greek cities.[14] Again, since Alexander's deed raises the presumption of an intention to interfere, the historian is obliged by that presumption to attribute to him a contrary intention. That attribution rests upon the unimpeached instructions to respect the cities' freedom.[15] The instructions are offered by

14. Tarn just previously states that "his object was two-fold. He wished to remove the danger to security involved in this floating mass of homeless men, ready to serve anyone as mercenaries. . . . He also entertained the impossible idea of putting an end to Greek faction-fights" (pp. 112–13). Still earlier, we are told that although Alexander restored autonomy to the cities freed from Persian domination, he nevertheless interfered (at Ephesus and Chios) for the limited purpose of putting an end to their civil warfare, favoring neither side: "This, common humanity apart, was a war measure, and has no bearing on the constitutional position of the cities . . ." (p. 33). It is reasonable to regard this as supporting Tarn's later claim, even though he does not allude to it at that place.

15. Actually, the picture is complicated by the need to understand and weigh a simultaneous deed of Alexander's, his request to the cities that he be deified. Tarn observes that deification had no religious import either for Alexander or for the cities, that "it was merely a political measure adopted for a limited political purpose, to give him, juridically, a foothold in autonomous Greek cities" (p. 114). What gives one pause is not the request itself but (I should expect) the implied compatibility, with a continuing and defensible belief in the integrity of his covenant with the league, of wanting this peculiar juridical foothold: "The Covenant bound Alexander of Macedon; it would not bind Alexander the god; the way therefore to exercise authority in the cities was to become a god. The exiles decree was therefore accompanied, or possibly even preceded, by a request to the cities of the League for his deification" (p. 113).

It is such a difficulty as this request creates which I had reference

Tarn as evidence that the deed was seen by Alexander as a response to an extraordinary and eliminable threat, and as such certainly not a commitment to the permanent abolition of that freedom. In addition, Tarn's claim that the instructions are evidence that the League was to continue as before implies that Alexander must have regarded the cities' opportunity of exercising that freedom to be unimpaired by the exceptional deed.

The actual success or failure of Tarn's brief does not matter, for our purpose. What matters is that his little argument mentions the *sort* of thing which can show that someone had or did not have a certain intention; that is, considerations showing that he could not, or could not but, have assigned a certain character to his deed. Such considerations are of matters of fact in the public domain, not at the disposal of the actor. (We know, for example, that when Alexander introduced the custom of prostration for all his subjects he knew that "to Greeks and Macedonians this did imply worship," and so for *that* reason we infer that he "must therefore have intended to become a god.") [16] Whether or not certain considerations make

---

to before in speaking of what makes problematic some claims as to what character may be assigned a certain deed.

16. *Ibid.*, p. 79. Here is another example, concerning a man who "danced challenge in front of the government soldiers who came to avenge the murder of the radjah in 1918. Exposing one's body to bullets with only a carabao shield as protection can be interpreted only as suicidal in intent" (Cora Du Bois, *The People of Alor: A Social-Psychological Study of an East Indian Island* [Minneapolis, 1944], p. 156). Earlier we have been introduced to the challenge dance, as one of "a number of more or less formalized outlets for anger that help to drain off the frustrations and humiliations associated with the social system" (p. 120).

Clear examples of the use of such considerations can be found even with respect to the troublesome area of an author's intentions. Waley, having characterized a Chinese prose work as an anti-bureau-

it even possible to take the deed in a certain way is open to the judgment of any relevantly knowledgeable person.

This is what accounts for a duplication in the underlying logic of these past two examples. The same relation holds between (a), Alexander's belief about the special nature of his decree, and (b), an intention therewith to break his word, as between (c), Pym's belief about constitutional and historical precedents, and (d), his having achieved a major constitutional innovation. In each case the belief serves to make intelligible (though not necessarily justified) the denial to the actor of the controversial characterization of his deed. And that which we take as showing whether or not there was, or even may have been, such a belief is not like the trout in Thoreau's milk. We are not limited even to excellent circumstantial evidence as to the possible nature of the belief.

---

cratic satire, defends his view in the following way: "The bureaucrats of the story are saints in Heaven, and it might be supposed that the satire was directed against religion rather than against bureaucracy. But the idea that the hierarchy in Heaven is a replica of government on earth is an accepted one in China. . . . In Chinese popular belief there is no ambiguity. Heaven is simply the whole bureaucratic system transferred bodily to the empyrean" (Wu Ch'eng-en, *Monkey,* trans. Arthur Waley [London, 1942], pp. 9–10).

I wish to emphasize that the point of these illustrations is to show what it is we commonly look to, in determining whether or not someone had a certain intention, or what intention he had. I have not claimed that by themselves they undermine every possible basis for philosophical skepticism as to the possibility, say, of ever knowing another's intentions. It is no accident, I must admit, that five otherwise diverse examples of confident ascription of a specified intention (namely, by Shapiro, Panofsky, Tarn, Du Bois, and Waley) have each concerned actions or achievements the characterization of which is extraordinarily dependent upon a special and socially-determined convention. But this peculiarity serves only to make the illustrations more telling. Its presence is no reason to impute a logical difference to cases lacking this feature.

One thing further emerges from this examination of the character-deed distinction and its implications. That is an elaboration of our original simple depiction of an intention as an action in prospect. It is apparent we now have a more informative way of putting this. When P intends S, S is a certain one (or set) of the characters of the deed.

It is that character P cannot credibly deny knowing the deed to have, given that he appreciates its character at such a time and in such circumstances as give him opportunity to act upon that appreciation, for example, to refrain from the deed. Both parts of this can be regarded as explications of the original formula. The first, as it were, attaches the deed's significant character to its author; it is *this* which is prospectively his. The second part insures that the deed, in that character, is chargeable to him as his action.[17]

17. In order, of course, to allow (e.g.) for negligent or involuntary acts, since time or circumstances can be such that one fully appreciates the character of the deed yet can fairly deny it was one's intention.

VII

Evidence of Intention

Part One

WHAT REMAINS is to give some consideration to such additional familiar aspects of our conception of intentions as may seem to be fit for articulation only in the vocabulary of the inner-state theorist. On the face of it, there is nothing calling for that kind of interpretation in the various ways we talk about our future intentions. For instance, the expression "an expression of intention" does not itself compel us to acknowledge a gap in time between the coming-into-being of the intention and that of the relevant deed. Here, the intention is the future deed, seen in a certain light. Problems about the expression of intention have to do not with the intention but with the expression, with one's routine ability now to declare what one will do and to differentiate such a declaration from other predictions of one's own future.

This is not to suggest that it is an easy matter even to state correctly what is genuinely problematic about utterances in the form, "I intend to. . . ." Consider this attempt to attach significance to a difference in grammatical person:

"I intend to . . ." is not simply the first person of the third person "he intended to. . . ." When I say "he intended to . . ." I describe something, perhaps his actions, perhaps his mental projects, perhaps both; but when I say "I intend to . . ." I do not describe anything at all. My intending is not something described or referred to by saying "I intend to . . ."; it simply *in one sense* is my saying "I intend to . . . ," whether I say this aloud or only think it.[1]

To begin with, the first sentence quoted has to be treated as elliptical, and in more than one respect, if it is to have any appearance of serving to make a true statement. MacIntyre wants to say rather that "I intend" is not simply the first person (singular indicative active) of "to intend." And since *that* is false, he wants this to be understood as a way of claiming that the speaker *does* something by an utterance using that verb in one person not done in the other; e.g., that by saying "I intend to . . ." he makes himself answerable for undertaking what is described in the subordinate infinitive. But now the second sentence ("When I say . . . ," etc.) undercuts even this plausible reconstruction, for the contrast drawn in that sentence is simply a false one. If "he intends [sic] to . . . ," as typically used, is a description, then so equally is "I intend to . . ."; if not, not. Presumably MacIntyre is beguiled in part by his inobservant, but significant, use of different tenses in drawing this alleged contrast. It would have given him pause

1. A. C. MacIntyre, *The Unconscious: A Conceptual Analysis* (London, 1958), p. 54.

to have attempted to express his claim about the first-person use in terms of "I intended. . . ."

The first part of the last sentence quoted is diagnostically welcome. It shows, in part, why MacIntyre supposes that what he says in the second sentence is true. For it is true that "I intend to . . ." in no way describes my 'intending', there being no such thing to be described. What, if anything, "I intend to . . ." describes is my intention. Yet "I intend" (as distinct from the infinitive) does not actually do that, either. By uttering it, I just tell you that what follows *is* my intention. At most, one could say that it bestows on what follows a certain status, that of a description of my intention.

Finally, the last part of that last sentence makes fully evident what impetus is behind the whole effort. That part ("it simply . . . ," etc.) does so despite its vanishing intelligibility; the statement, "My intending is my saying 'I intend to . . .'," is one we can at best concede to be false.[2] MacIntyre's misapprehension is that "to intend" is strictly comparable to Austin's paradigm verbs of performatory utterance. The first sentence, in effect, is a claim that it can be placed in that select company, and the second and third sentences attempt to back up the claim, to persuade us that by saying "I intend," I do (in one sense).

All of this is put forward in a good cause. MacIntyre wants to deny us the cheap way out of a supposed dilemma. It has been asserted there are equal reasons for saying both that an intention is essentially "a piece of mental planning" and that it is nothing but a coherent pattern (or the gratifying endpoint of a pattern) of "outward action." MacIntyre anticipates

2. No matter how emphatic the promissory gesture to other 'senses'. Moreover, in one sense of what? "My intending"? "Is"?

the easy response, insisting that "it will not do simply to suggest that the one model is appropriate for some types of situation, the other for others." But in the course of this he concedes that "sometimes we discover a man's intentions by asking him what they are and sometimes by observing his behaviour and sometimes by both. . . ."[3] We are to understand, I take it, that whenever one passes from ignorance of another's intentions to knowledge of them, one of these three forms of report is warranted. By one route or another, the passage, if made, is always that of discovery.

Yet this is not so. It is a strongly suggestive falsehood to contrast (i) someone's telling us what he will do, with (ii) observation, say, of (what we take to be) a coherent and unfinished course of action he is pursuing. Though it may be acceptable to say that we *learn* what he will do from his saying what he will do, it is not generally the case that we *discover* his intention by means of attending to his utterance. At least, learning of his intention in this normal way is not strictly comparable to the kind of penetration achieved by *interpreting* some body of gestures, acts, and expressions so as to discover what hitherto had been concealed by the uninterpreted 'behavioral' materials. This being so, there is no initial requirement even to deal with this supposed embarrassment of equally well-attested but divergent models of intentional action.

Just as there is nothing in the fact that we can ahead of time say what our intentions are which prima facie demands the identification of a certain inner state as the intention, so neither is there any singular problem in understanding accounts of the thwarting or abandonment of an intention. Such accounts tell us of what would otherwise have been done, not of the passing out of existence of a once-real thing, the intention.

3. *The Unconscious*, p. 54.

Still, it will be useful to take note of a related sort of experience. There are cases in which the action *does* go through, a deed is done, which yet are such that the actor himself would describe the whole episode as one in which what transpired was in some way seriously incongruent with his intention. These deserve notice because the bare fact of their existence could lead one reasonably (because precipitately) to infer the reality of some categorial distinction of action and intention. These are cases different, it should be observed, from that reported of Pym, which was an instance of a conflict between the character given the deed by the actor and that assigned by the spectator (the historian).

Consideration of two actual cases may be sufficient to abort such an inference. They are both instances of someone's *doing* what he wanted, if you like, yet finding the upshot different from the intention. In the first, we are told that as a consequence of the League of Nation's condemnation of Italy's move in Abyssinia, "The Stresa front was gone beyond recognition, Mussolini forced on to the German side. In attacking Abyssinia, Mussolini had intended to exploit the international tension on the Rhine, not to opt for Germany. Instead he lost his freedom of choice." [4] The second narrative is more arresting, because in it the historian says flatly that the outcome was the opposite of the actor's intention. This appears in an account of the British part in events leading up to the Munich agreement:

Their motives [in raising the Czechoslovak question] were of the highest. They wished to prevent a European war. They wished also to achieve a settlement more in accordance with the great principles of self-determination than that made in 1919. The outcome

4. A. J. P. Taylor, *The Origins of the Second World War* (London, 1961), p. 108.

was the precise opposite of their intention. They imagined that there was a "solution" of the Sudeten German problem and that negotiations would produce it. In fact the problem was insoluble in terms of compromise and every step in negotiations only made this clearer. By seeking to avert a crisis, the British brought it on.[5]

There is an economic way of showing the accommodation of such accounts to our previous analysis; namely, to recognize that they could be rephrased in terms of P's doing S with the intention that T (or, of doing T). This construction is one of the most common ways in which the substantive actually occurs, as when it is said (e.g.) that Colonel Blood entered the Tower with the intention of stealing the regalia. I suggest that no more definite characterization of what this phrase achieves can be given than that it says that T (for example, stealing the regalia) must be viewed as the anticipated terminus of S. There is a certain attraction to a more substantial alternative. Yet that proves to be plainly unsatisfactory, when put to the test. The alternative would be to say that T is thereby positioned in the account as a *direct* (perhaps understood as a causal) outcome of doing S. But often, and naturally, T cancels out S, or restores the initial situation changed by doing S (as when, e.g., it is said that Hearn sailed for Japan with the intention of returning).

Now, it is a fair summary of part of the longer narrative quoted to say that therein we are told that the British government initiated formal discussion on the Sudetenland question with the intention of averting a war crisis. Accordingly, let us say that their deed was that of initiating certain diplomatic discussions and that the intention to which the historian refers was that of averting a crisis. The critical point, with respect to the theoretical inference in question, comes when we pick out

5. *Ibid.*, p. 155.

the deed to which the narrative attaches that intention, as its character. And here the relevant deed is *not* the one already mentioned, that of initiating the negotiations. Rather, the intention of averting a crisis is the character attached to the anticipated *result* of that deed, namely, the satisfaction of the last apparent major source of German territorial grievance.

Similarly, the situation which Mussolini is said not to have wanted is not that of having attacked Abyssinia, but rather that of having thereby sacrificed Italy's previous relative freedom of choosing from among alternative places in European power alignments. Thus neither of these cases, when accurately described, can be said to turn upon a differentiation of the thing done from what *it* was intended to be. The differentiation is of the actual from the anticipated character of the *outcome* (here, the result) of the whole course of events in which the thing done is placed.

Actually, there is a bit more complexity built into the specimen about Mussolini, and it should be taken care of if the case made on the basis of the example is to be well made. The complication is this: the wording of the second sentence ("In attacking Abyssinia. . . ," etc.) may seem to pit (a) exploiting the international tension on the Rhine, against (b) opting for an alliance with Germany, as competing candidates for the role of the character of the deed of attacking Abyssinia. But this is not so. It is clearly (a) which is a characterization of that deed, whereas (b) is a possible outcome of so acting. In a way, therefore, this specimen is different from the Munich case. The difference, of no consequence to the argument, can be put by saying that while the British action failed to have an outcome they anticipated and desired (and indeed had an outcome they positively did not want), the account of Mussolini's action tells us more simply that it had an outcome which it is not the case he had wanted. No *anticipation* of an outcome is attributed to Mussolini, contrary to what is said of the British.

Part Two

There is outstanding one more potentially troublesome fact. We shall deal with it here, though only briefly. That is the fact that sometimes accounts of human actions are built upon a contrast between an overt act and an intention. The overt act is often said to be a sign of a certain intention. Thus one's appreciation of what it is for something to be *evidence* of a person's intention will be affected by one's grasp of the notion of an overt act, and of the consequent relation of an act so designated to an intention. We shall look at this relation. In the course of so doing, we can also touch upon the neglected notion of sincerity. As before, the analysis will hang upon a few instructive cases.

What needs recognition first is a negative feature. That which makes an act overt is not some characteristic attributable to the act independently of reference to an intention, purpose, or the like. It is not the case that an act is overt in virtue, say, of literally being exposed in the public streets. Rather, to call an act overt is at least tacitly to indicate that it is taken as enjoying a certain relation (e.g.) to an intention. Here is a standard example of such an indication:

What was . . . urgently needed was a settlement with the Miura family, which . . . had for some years been ill-disposed towards the Hojo family. . . . Tokiyori [regent, and of the Hojo family] had no convincing evidence that the Miura intended to attack him. . . . In this uneasy situation Tokiyori remained on the alert but took no action. He seems to have been waiting for some overt act by the Miura family, which would justify reprisals on a large scale.[6]

Now, any conception of an overt act will provide for its utility as (somehow) an index of intention. To obtain a correct conception, we must look for the specific way in which an act, in this instance, would overtly have shown the inimical intention of the Miura family. A further test of that conception is the character it implicitly assigns to covert acts.

Is there any way in which an act *could* be convincing evidence of a certain intention? Of course there is, if the act bears the relation to the intention of a sample to a lode. So in the instance at hand, an act could have been regarded as overt, relative to the intention in question, only if it was a deed having the character named (i.e., an attack) which the Miura could credibly neither deny having undertaken or sponsored, nor deny having in advance appreciated as an attack (or, at least, as prelude). Given this explication of what it is which would make an act overt, there emerges what could have made one covert, relative to that intention. That is, that the act could have been such that it might reasonably have been seen as one of the significant kind (in this situation, attack or preparation for attack), but was not prima facie such.

Note that, on this sketch of these notions, an act remains overt even if unappreciated, and covert even when exposed. Such indeed is the case. It is worth identifying emphatically *what* it is that achieves the concealment, since it is not (say) physical barriers in and of themselves, the dark of night or silence of conspiracy. Nor is it the theorist's favorite, the gap from material to spiritual substance. If any one sort of thing

6. G. B. Sansom, *A History of Japan to 1334* (Stanford, 1958), p. 409.

may be singled out to play this role, it is misappreciation of the deed. Normally, of course, the chance of making such a mistake is enhanced, even insured, by stealth and other arts. But it need not be, for one to enjoy the opportunity of being misapprehended.[7] Further, it should be said that the potential for such misapprehension is not always a creative contribution on the part of either actor or spectator. The deed may occur in such a context, or be complex in such a way, as positively to mislead an onlooker, or at least to preclude confident assessment of the evidence before him.[8]

We may now bring the topic of an individual's sincerity into this exploration of evidence of intention. Here is an account parsimoniously connecting disproof of a certain intention with disproof of that actor's sincerity:

Everything depended on the King's good faith, and Pym . . . was unwilling to believe in it. For him, the Irish army was the touchstone of the King's sincerity. He may or may not have believed that Strafford had seriously advocated using that army against the

7. Consider this account, especially useful in that the physical concealment mentioned in the episode is so plainly not what accounts for the spectators' mistake: "On Sundays he used to shut his children in a barn. To his devout neighbours . . . this must have seemed an admirable practice. But in fact the minister's motives were less orthodox. He shut his family in a barn not to punish them, but to give them a place where they could play together, safe from the censorious eyes of his parishioners" (Robert Blake, *The Life and Times of Andrew Bonar Law, 1858–1923: Prime Minister of the United Kingdom* [New York, 1956], p. 20).

8. See, for example, C. H. V. Sutherland, *Coinage in Roman Imperial Policy, 31 B.C.–A.D. 68* (London, 1951), pp. 109–10. This is an account, concerning the Senate's attempt to predict from his early deeds in office what Caligula's intentions were with respect to the Augustan restrictions on that office, which nicely illustrates how a body of circumstances and deeds may be such as to hamper inference from evidence to intention.

English. But he certainly believed that the King could only dis-
prove such an intention on his own part by disbanding the Irish
army.[9]

Again, it must be established that this demand for disproof of
an intention is not a claim that the occurrence of a certain
action would (somehow) show that a certain inner episode
had *not* occurred. That the demand is not such a claim can
easily be shown. Relative to the intention in question here, the
act demanded of Charles (that of disbanding the army then
in Ireland) is just the converse of the overt act referred to in
the preceding case, relative to the hostile intention in question
there. For in the present instance the action would be such
that its commission would *preclude* Charles' then doing any
deed to which the significant character, 'using that army
against the English', could be assigned.

In Pym's eyes, for Charles even to permit the continued
existence of that potential instrument for bringing Parliament
to heel would be to show his insincerity in having protested
the charge of a hostile intention toward Parliament. On this
account of how matters stood at that moment, the king's an-
tagonists would in effect have argued that Charles' failure to
act (i.e., to disband that army) would itself virtually have
been an overt act, a deed the king could not honestly deny
having seen as one of threatening his critics in England.[10]

9. C. V. Wedgwood, *The King's Peace* (New York, 1956), p. 420.
10. Here is another and even stronger example of how it is that our
reasons for basing an attribution of insincerity on certain actions can
be facts to which the actor does not have sole access: "There is a simple
test of the sincerity of Mussolini's apparently reasonable talk about
revisionism [concerning World War I treaty settlements] in the fact
that he always made it clear that revisionism might apply to others
but in no circumstances to Italy: [Italy's gains] were established facts,
irrevocable decisions, about which he would expatiate with fervor,

The general point about the grounds on which a charge of insincerity can be based is this: what a man does (conditions permitting) stands as the test of the sincerity of his prior avowal of intention, not as a product is indicative of the nature of the efficient cause which produced it, but, again, as an assay tells the content of a reputed lode, or a journey the accuracy of a hearsay map. His sincerity is shown by the match of the undeniable character of his actual deed with that of his predicted deed. To see this, however, is to see just the rudiments of the concept of sincerity in action.

To speak of the expression of an intention as the prediction of a deed is, of course, argumentative. In doing so I mean at least to commit myself to the rejection of a certain viewpoint, one according to which the expression of an intention has essentially to do with one's condition at the time of declaring the intention. Richard Price, again, provides a nicely ambiguous expression of this viewpoint, in saying that "when I say I *intend* to do an action, I affirm only a present fact." [11] Taken from its context this remark certainly admits of a favorable interpretation, namely, as the statement that when I say truly that I intend to do such-and-such, it is a fact at the time of utterance that I intend to do so. But seen in its context it is plain Price's remark is meant in a different, and paradoxical, way. For at that place he is struggling to say what promising involves, and he adopts the tactic of contrasting it with the

---

even calling to his aid the sanctity of the signature on a treaty" (René Albrecht-Carrié, *Italy from Napoleon to Mussolini* [New York, 1960], p. 204). Except at the price of manifesting severe self-deception, Mussolini could not credibly have claimed not to recognize his implicit self-contradiction. Either way such a man has forfeited the standing of a rational participant.

11. *A Review of the Principal Questions in Morals,* ed. D. D. Raphael (Oxford, 1948), p. 155.

act of expressing one's intention. He says, allowably, that "a promise must mean more than" merely "declaring a *resolution* or *intention*"; he then unacceptably finds that "the whole difference is, that the one relates to the *present,* the other to *future* time." The paradoxical import of this is bare, for example in his statement that "after declaring a resolution to do an action, a man is under no obligation actually to do it, because *he did not say he would.*" [12]

It is important here to note further only that the diverse particular ways in which judgment of the sincerity of someone's expression of intention is made difficult can all be said to have one source. That source is the difficulty, at times, of discovering just what was the character assigned by the actor to the deed, however admissible its assignment as a possible character of that deed. It is a failure, or inability, of this sort which accounts for honestly mistaken attributions of insincerity. For example, it is only reasonable to judge that a person

12. *Ibid.* (last emphasis added). There are still other passages in which Price gives lucid expression to the inner-state view of intentions and the consequent implication that our actions are only contingently significant indices of them. For example: *"External actions* are to be considered as signs of *internal actions,* or of the motives and views of agents" (p. 200).

It should be noted that there are considerable local variations among adherents to what I have been calling the standard view. One important example is provided by J. S. Mill. In defending the 'objectivity' of the Utilitarian standard, he is in one place moved to insist upon the importance, for ethics, of distinguishing intentions from motives, the specific nature of the latter being irrelevant to assessing the morality of the action. Mill here calls an intention "what the agent *wills to do,*" whereas a motive remains, in his eyes, something clearly inner and episodic, "the feeling which makes him will to do so." This is in a long footnote to the second chapter of *Utilitarianism,* appearing only in the second edition (see the edition by Oskar Piest [New York, 1957], p. 24, n. 3).

must be insincere who denies the king the right to choose his ministers and yet himself is eager for such appointment by the king's heir. Yet a recent authoritative critic of historical work on George III is at pains to argue, contrary to the formidable implication by Namier, that "we must beware of assuming that Fox would be sincere in the latter case (as though this were his realist policy) but insincere in the former case, as though it represented the mere "programme" of an opposition. . . ." [13] Among several considerations the historian deploys to reverse this judgment, the most weighty is the factual claim that "it was possible for the Whigs to feel that the King was in harmony with the will of the nation when he brought them into office, but not when he appointed the Tory supporters of the royal prerogative." [14] Whether one accepts this claim, and gives it the same weight as does Butterfield, is of little consequence here. What matters is the *domain* of considerations within which the argument moves. Both defense and discovery of one's sincerity in declaring a certain intention turn upon evidence, such as even this intricate claim, which is in the public domain.

13. Herbert Butterfield, *George III and the Historians,* rev. ed. (New York, 1959), p. 256.
14. *Ibid.* For an even more manifold rebuttal of a charge of insincerity in declaring one's intention, see J. S. Watson, *The Reign of George III, 1760–1815* (*The Oxford History of England,* Vol. XII) (Oxford, 1960), pp. 402–3. This defense of Pitt against the undeniably plausible accusation of duplicity toward the Irish is that the accusation is "false to the facts of the situation," facts the articulation of which amounts to an extremely complex recharacterization of the intention in question.

Index

Index